It has become a tired cliché to say that folk have to check their brains at the door when they enter a church. Nothing could be further from the truth. Christianity has never set faith against reason, and neither do the contributors to this book. No one who reads these intellectual testimonies with an open mind could fairly draw the conclusion that Christianity is rationally indefensible or irrelevant in the modern world. The authors faithfully fulfil the apostle Peter's exhortation to give the reason for the hope that they have in Christ.

James Anderson
Associate Professor of Theology and Philosophy, Reformed Theological Seminary
Charlotte, North Carolina

We have long needed a book in which several well-qualified Christians give intelligent, courteously-expressed reasons why atheism is bankrupt, then testify to the unique integrity and relevance of Christianity. *This is it!* Read it, pass it on — then get more copies and repeat the process!

John Blanchard
Internationally-known Christian preacher, teacher, apologist and author
Surrey, England

The conscious and purposeful choice of atheism as a creed (and as an active and militant creed) is becoming a notable feature of western culture today. Usually atheists claim to hold to their position as a matter of consistent logic, reason, science and compelling weighing of evidence, while it is Christians who are considered (often in a very disparaging way) simply to have embraced 'blind faith' which ignores all these.

This book, however, presents considered arguments from eleven intelligent, thinking people from a range of professional spheres, each of whom argues persuasively (and politely) why in their eyes atheism has been found intellectually wanting. They have either abandoned or rejected atheism for very good reasons.

No doubt there are some closed-minded atheists who simply will not want to engage with a book like this. But for the many honest, open-minded sceptics who do want to reasonably weigh all the evidence, this book will be thought-provoking, stimulating and perhaps even life-changing.

William J U Philip
Senior Minister, The T̶ ̶ ̶ ̶ ̶ ̶ ̶ ̶ ̶ ̶ ̶ ̶ ̶ gist
̶ ̶ ̶ nd

With Atheism having well and truly arrived as the new kid on the block in today's secular society, this book is a valuable resource for all who take the big questions of life seriously. Neither academic in style, nor polemic in tone, it combines good-going apologetics with the narrative of personal stories, all in a thoroughly readable and always engaging way: believers will be emboldened, doubters fortified, and atheists warmly challenged!

Jeremy Middleton

Minister, Davidson's Mains Parish Church and Chairman of the Crieff Trust

Edinburgh, Scotland

Each of the contributors brings a warmth and rigour that is both personal and fully engaged with the questions our world – and our hearts – ask. This book will help your heart rejoice in the God who is Lord over every square inch of his creation, and whose word is trustworthy and true.

Mark Ellis

Team Leader for Scotland, UCCF:thechristianunions

Dundee, Scotland

WHY I AM NOT AN ATHEIST

FACING THE INADEQUACIES OF UNBELIEF

EDITED BY DAVID J. RANDALL

SOLAS
CENTRE FOR PUBLIC CHRISTIANITY

CHRISTIAN
FOCUS

David J. Randall has been in ministry for more than forty years and is presently locum minister in the newly-formed Grace Church, Dundee. He is also Vice-chairman of the Board of Solas – Centre for Public Christianity.

Copyright © David J. Randall 2013

paperback ISBN 978-1-78191-270-6
epub ISBN 978-1-78191-308-6
Mobi ISBN 978-1-78191-309-3

10 9 8 7 6 5 4 3 2 1

Published in 2013
by
Christian Focus Publications Ltd,
Geanies House, Fearn,
Ross-shire, IV20 1TW, Scotland.
www.christianfocus.com

with

Solas – CPC
Dundee, Scotland
www.solas-cpc.org

Cover design by
Daniel van Straaten

Printed by
Bell and Bain, Glasgow

CONTENTS

PREFACE

The title of this book may seem somewhat negative! Its writers would all say that they are Christians for positive reasons – it is not principally a matter of what we are not, but of what we are (or what we believe we have been led to). It should be said at the outset that the main thrust of the chapters that follow is not that atheism is untenable for different reasons and, therefore, we have all been driven into Christian belief as a kind of last resort. Our Christianity is much more positive than that!

I have often reflected on the comment of a professor who was returning a student's essay in which the student had been dismissive of a certain theory. The professor wrote in the margin, 'Every theory has its difficulties, but you have not considered whether any other theory has less difficulties than the one you have criticised.'[1] Both atheism and theism have their difficulties; in our finite existence we simply do not have all the answers to all the questions that may be posed, and in one sense we must look for the 'philosophy' that has fewest difficulties.

So far as Christianity is concerned, no one would claim that as believers we have all the answers; Deuteronomy 29:29 says that

---

1   J. Baillie, *Invitation to Pilgrimage* (Oxford University Press, 1942), p. 15.

some things have been revealed for us and succeeding generations but there are other things that are secret and belong to God alone. There are many areas in which we do not have the answers and sometimes 'I don't know' is the appropriate response to some questions that can be posed.

However, as Pascal wrote: 'Everything that cannot be understood does nevertheless not cease to exist'[2], and our conviction is that fewer difficulties attach to Christian belief than to atheism. In saying that we are convinced Christians, we are not claiming to have everything 'sussed out', but we believe that atheism has far too many weaknesses to be an option.

In this preface, we would emphasize two things about our subject. The first is that we do not regard our faith as something we have worked out or even discovered for ourselves. Jesus once said to His disciples: 'You did not choose me, but I chose you' (John 15:16), and those who believe in Him today regard the matter in this way. The eighteenth-century poet Josiah Conder expressed it devotionally in verse:

My Lord, I did not choose You,
For that could never be;
This heart would still refuse You,
Had You not chosen me.
My heart knows none above You;
For You I long, I thirst
And know that if I love You,
Lord, You have loved me first.

Those who profess to be committed Christians do not attribute that faith to any moral or intellectual abilities of their own. Far from that, they say, 'To God be the glory – great things He has done.'

We also believe that our Creator has given us free will and we are called to respond in one way or another to the invitation of Christ in His gospel. However, once that decision has been made, the believer is increasingly conscious of having only responded

---

2   Blaise Pascal, *Pensées* (Oxford World Classics edition, 1995), p. 79.

to the initiative of Another. There will always, we believe, remain a mystery in this matter (holding together belief in divine sovereignty and human free will), but those who believe would say that the principal and overarching reason why we are not atheists is that God has revealed Himself to us.[3] In the profound words which C. S. Lewis put into the mouth of Aslan (representing Christ): 'You would not have called to me unless I had been calling to you.'[4]

We do not claim any kind of superiority to anyone else and, in writing about this subject, we begin from the point of being grateful to the God whose grace and mercy extends to the undeserving and the unworthy. In fact, our great hope and prayer is that this little book may be an instrument in the hands of the God we trust and that He might use it to lead others to put their faith and trust in Him, so that they too might be no longer atheists but believers in Jesus Christ. It is simply (as an often-quoted aphorism has it) one beggar telling another beggar where food is to be found.

The other introductory thing we would say is that we do not approach this subject with any kind of belligerence or aggression, much less hatred, towards people who would describe themselves as atheists, especially people who have given serious attention to the issues and remain unconvinced of the truth of theism and/or Christianity.

We do not wish to reply in kind to the aggressive and sometimes vitriolic attacks on faith that are found in some of today's 'new atheism' which is often quite fundamentalist (to use a word they love to level at us) in its dogmatic unbelief and which is sometimes remarkably intolerant of those who are, as they would say, so silly and naive as to 'still' believe nowadays.

Some of these attacks are irrational and some are belligerent. Jonathan Sacks has drawn attention to the latter in the following manner:

---

3   'This is the grace that brought Zaccheus into the sycamore tree to await the Saviour; the grace that brought Lydia to the riverside where she was to hear of the Saviour and have her heart opened; the grace that took Onesimus to Rome to meet with the messenger of the cross that he might be free for ever.' – R. A. Finlayson, *Reformed Theological Writings* (Christian Focus, 1996), p. 93.

4   C. S. Lewis, *The Silver Chair* (Puffin Books, 1965 edition), p. 28.

[T]he new atheism has launched an unusually aggressive attack on religion, which is not good for religion, for science, for intellectual integrity or for the future of the West. When a society loses its religion, it tends not to last very long thereafter. It discovers that having severed the ropes that moor its morality to something transcendent, all it has left is relativism, and relativism is incapable of defending anything including itself. When a society loses its soul, it is about to lose its future.[5]

It's an interesting comment from the Chief Rabbi of the United Kingdom, and we could argue with the implied notion (as expressed in Joseph's song in *The Amazing Technicolor Dreamcoat*) that '*any* dream will do', but Sacks certainly underlines the crucial importance of having a transcendent foundation for social and ethical values.

One of these Christian values is that of not repaying evil for evil (Rom. 12:17) – which in turn reflects the famous words of Jesus that His followers should 'turn the other cheek' (Matt. 5:39). We are called to love our fellow human beings, and one of the greatest expressions of love is the desire to share what we believe is the best good news ever.

The writer of the elaborately constructed Psalm 119, spoke about rejoicing in God's truth as one who finds great treasure (Ps. 119:162) and, in terms of a parable Jesus told, we feel like the pearl merchant who has come upon the most precious stone he has ever seen (Matt. 13:45). This is the context and the mood in which we present these reasons why we are not atheists but believers in Jesus Christ.

So, even as we write against the background of the so-called 'new atheism', with its sometimes irrational belligerence and lack of all deference and respect (and even tolerance), we would begin by emphasizing our desire not to belittle or deride anyone.

As we seek to explain why we are not atheists, we emphasize again that we do not wish to be negative. It is not just that we are *not* atheists but that we *are* Christians. We have positive reasons for believing, and the main reason why we are not atheists is that

---

5   Jonathan Sacks, *The Great Partnership* (Hodder & Stoughton, 2011), p. 2.

we are persuaded of the truth of Christianity. We find Christian faith and discipleship not only convincing but also wonderfully liberating and life-enhancing.

Our title obviously alludes to that of Bertrand Russell's famous lecture/publication, originally delivered back in 1927, and some chapters will refer specifically to Russell's arguments there. Our situation now, however, is more pressing than it was then, because of the current lack of common courtesy and respect for views that have held sway, at least in public life, for many centuries. We can no longer assume that Christianity will be even the default position of our society and there is a great need for more people who can 'give a reason' for the faith they hold (1 Pet. 3:15) and who can, 'with gentleness and respect', show the truth and the relevance of that faith in a world badly in need of it, a world in which we 'watch while sanity dies, touched by madness and lies'.[6]

The essays which follow have been contributed by people who are members or friends of Solas, the Centre for Public Christianity, based in Dundee, Scotland.[7] We gave writers freedom to develop the theme in their own ways and each writes from his or her particular perspective and background in terms of personal and professional experience.

The eleven writers[8] are varied in nationality, age, gender, life-experience and faith-story. Some respond to the notion that it has only been their upbringing or environment that has made them believers, and one to the charge that the reason why he is not an atheist is that he is paid to preach Christ! Some write about their experience of what it was to be an atheist, of being involved in a spiritual search and of having their faith tested by life's trials. We have instances of people coming to faith from backgrounds in journalism, psychiatry and science – with the very first chapter beginning provocatively: 'I am a scientist and I think like one. That is one of the main reasons that I am not an atheist.'

---

6   From the hymn, *Great is the darkness* by Graham Kendrick, 1992.

7   http://www.solas-cpc.org

8   The chapters are arranged in alphabetical order of authors' surnames.

Solas is all about seeking to bring the good news of Jesus into the context of twenty-first-century European culture. In response to those who would exclude Christianity from the public arena, we want to promote the positive teaching and example of Christ. As our website says, we believe that Europe was founded upon and largely owes its culture and existence to Christianity and that the rejection of Christianity in favour of an ill-defined and untried secular humanism is at best a plunge into dangerous waters, and at worst, a return to the Dark Ages.

Shortly after Jesus was born at Bethlehem, old Simeon said: '[For] my eyes have seen your salvation, which you have prepared in the sight of all people' (Luke 2:30-31) – on which Matthew Henry commented: 'It is ... not to be hid in a corner, but to be made known.'[9] Solas (as our website says)

> seeks to promote vigorous public engagement on many fronts. Christianity is applicable to every area of modern life and through the development of differing focus areas we will seek to demonstrate how public engagement can happen. We will encourage Christians and churches to use the arts, philosophy, music, history, society, media, medicine, science, theology and the community of the church, to express and teach the Christian faith, as given to us in the Scriptures of the Old and New Testaments.

The Archbishop of Canterbury has referred to the appointment of a United States Supreme Court justice about whom a senator commented that the man's (Roman Catholic) faith would not be a problem as long as it did not affect his opinions! 'You might think', Dr Justin Welby went on, 'that that was so improbably absurd as to be howled down with hysterical laughter, but it was not; it was seen as a serious comment.' In his first speech after being named as Archbishop, Dr Welby 'urged Christians not to be afraid to refer to their faith, despite an assumption that they should "excise" their beliefs from their minds when holding public positions.'[10]

---

9   Matthew Henry's *Commentary on the Whole Bible* (Hendrickson edition, 2012), p. 1458.

10   http://www.telegraph.co.uk/news/9679324/Christians-should-not-be-afraid-to-refer-to-their-faith-says-new-Archbishop.html.

There have been several recent examples of bizarre attitudes in such matters. In a high-profile case in Britain, a nurse was disciplined – not for some serious malpractice or negligence – but for offering to pray for a sick patient! Thankfully, she was later reinstated, but what a terrible thing she had done! The broadcaster Jeremy Vine has said that he feels pressure to avoid talking about Christianity on his shows; he feels that Christians are becoming outcasts and that the country is increasingly intolerant of 'religion'.

Early in 2012 it was reported that the National Secular Society, along with a local atheist ex-councillor, has sued Bideford Town Council in Devon over the issue of prayers at the beginning of council meetings. The High Court ruled that local councils have no lawful powers to hold prayers during official business – although, in response, the UK Government has written to local councils, telling them that new laws restore their power to hold prayers at official meetings. 'Intolerant secularism' is the phrase used by Eric Pickles, the Secretary of State for Local Government, to describe the secularist agenda, as he expressed the view that Britain has not been strengthened by the secularization of civil life.[11]

During 2011, the 400th anniversary of the publication of the Authorized Version of the Bible was celebrated, and Melvyn Bragg wrote a book about its influence. The preface gives quotations from several reviews; these include references to people who 'wish to banish religion from public life' (*The Independent*) and others for whom it is 'fashionable to deride or dismiss the Christian tradition' (*The Scotsman*).[12] This is the climate in which Christianity needs to reassert its place not as a private pursuit for the religiously minded, but as public truth which is of enormous relevance for social, political, commercial and educational life as well as for private life. Christianity did not start 'in a corner' (Acts 26:26) and it must not be kept in a corner now.

---

11   Information taken from *Christian Institute News*, 24th February 2012.

12   Both quoted in the frontispiece to *The Book of Books* (Hodder & Stoughton, 2011).

Notes on Contributors

DONALD BRUCE is managing director of the ethics consultancy *Edinethics Ltd*. He holds doctorates in chemistry and theology. From 1976 to 1992 he worked in nuclear energy research, safety and risk regulation, and Government energy policy. From 1992 to 2007 he was Director of the Church of Scotland's *Society, Religion and Technology Project* (SRT), pioneering the examination of ethical and societal issues in emerging technologies, notably on GM crops and animals, cloning and stem cells, and nanotechnologies. He has also worked on the ethics of technological risk, gene patenting, sustainable development and climate policy. He is a regular speaker, writer and broadcaster on bioethics nationally and internationally. He is also much involved in public participation in science, especially with the New Economics Foundation.

ALISTAIR DONALD has a doctorate in environmental science (University of Wales) and worked in that field for a number of years in Wales and Scotland before being called to the ministry. After training at New College in Edinburgh, he served for ten years as parish minister in New Deer, Aberdeenshire. In 2009 he became Chaplain to Heriot-Watt University. A former convener of the Scottish Churches Apologetics Committee, he has also been a member of the SRT project's Synthetic Biology working group. He has a long-standing interest in the relation of science and faith, and has lectured and debated on the subject in a variety of church, university and public contexts. He is married to Nicky and they have three grown sons.

HENK DROST was born in 1953 in Holland. He is a missionary child who lived for six years in Papua where his father worked as a missionary; since then he has been interested in aviation. After studies at the University of the Reformed Churches in Holland and the Institute for Reformed Theological Training, he served four congregations in Holland and from 1990 to 1998 worked also as an evangelist (church planter) in the south of Holland. He was a member of the Board of the Theological University in Kampen and was also a member and chairman of the deputies for church planting in Holland and Belgium. He is a member of the Assistance Board of the Evangelical Presbyterian Churches in Austria and Switzerland. He has published some booklets and articles on evangelism and ecclesiology. Since 2007 he has worked in Ukraine as a missionary for the Dutch Reformed Mission to support the Ukrainian Evangelical Reformed Churches. He is married to Ria and they have six children and eight grandchildren.

ELAINE DUNCAN is the Chief Executive of the Scottish Bible Society which supports Bible work (translation, production and distribution) around the world and seeks to encourage Bible engagement in Scotland. Elaine is enthusiastic about people having a Bible in their own language, and helping people understand it and grow in their relationship with Jesus Christ through it. Elaine's previous employment was with Scripture Union Scotland (eleven years) and the Universities and Colleges Christian Fellowship (fourteen years). She has a degree in Behavioural Sciences (psychology) and worked for eighteen months in a psychiatric unit. The focus of Elaine's work has always been to encourage people to know God better as they interact with His Word. Her involvement with national events such as the Keswick Convention and Spring

Harvest has been an expression of this. Elaine is originally from Cumbria but now lives in Glasgow, works in Edinburgh and supports the Scottish rugby team!

ALEX MACDONALD has been a minister of the Free Church of Scotland for more than forty years, but his journey was somewhat unconventional. As a 1960s teenager, Alex was the first 'hippy' minister in the Free Church. Long hair, beards and outrageous clothes aside, Alex officially began serving God in Bishopbriggs, running outreach cafes and youth clubs during the 1970s. By the 1980s, he was ministering in Aberdeen – a period of great church growth among students and young people – and heading up the burgeoning Free Church Camps work. He is now minister of Buccleuch Church in Edinburgh. He is knowledgeable on church and civil law, has served on Lothian Region and Edinburgh City Education Committees and has published several books and released CDs of his music. He has also served as Free Church Media Officer and Editor of *The Monthly Record*. Alex's main interests lie in developing communication of the gospel, trying to understand his grandchildren, playing football, climbing Scottish mountains, writing songs, and singing and playing in a band.

PABLO MARTINEZ is a medical doctor and psychiatrist working currently at a private practice in Barcelona. He has also developed a wide ministry as a lecturer, counsellor and itinerant speaker. He has been a plenary Bible teacher in more than thirty countries in Europe and the Americas. He was a member of the Executive Committee of the International Christian Medical and Dental Association for twenty years (1986-2006), also serving as one of the organization's vice-presidents. He has been President of the Spanish Evangelical Alliance (1999-2009) and was Professor of Pastoral Psychology at the Spanish Theological Seminary for seven years. He is currently the leader of the European Christian Counsellors Network, a body connected to the European Leadership Forum. He has authored three books: *Praying with the Grain: How Your Personality Affects the Way You Pray* (Monarch Books, 2012, now published in fourteen languages); *Tracing the Rainbow: Walking Through Loss*

17

and Bereavement (Authentic Media/Spring Harvest, 2004); and *A Thorn in the Flesh: Finding strength and hope amid suffering* (IVP, 2007). Pablo is married to Marta, also a medical doctor. Bird-watching and reading are two of his main hobbies.

DAVID RANDALL, after studies in Edinburgh and Princeton, ministered in Macduff, Aberdeenshire, from 1971 – 2010, during which time he preached through all of the books of the Bible. He also served as convener of 'Why Believe?' His publications include *believe it or not* (answering objections to the Christian faith) and a missionary biography, *Grace Sufficient*. He wrote a fortnightly newspaper column, *It Makes You Think,* for about 25 years. He is married to Nan, and they have three sons (two of whom are also pastors), a daughter and six grandchildren. In retirement, apart from swimming and jogging, he is locum pastor at Grace Church, Dundee and is also vice-chairman of the Solas Board of Trustees.

DAVID ROBERTSON is the minister of St Peter's Free Church in Dundee, Scotland (a church that is best known for being the church of Robert Murray McCheyne). He is the author of *Awakening* (a contemporary account of McCheyne's life) and *The Dawkins Letters*. The latter has resulted in his being invited to debate and discuss all over the United Kingdom and elsewhere in Europe. This has been done in cafes, bars, libraries, universities, pubs, restaurants, village halls – and even occasionally churches! David is a chaplain at the University of Dundee and Director of the Solas Centre for Public Christianity. His *Magnificent Obsession* has been published and he is also working on an evangelistic book on *Ecclesiastes*. He is married to Annabel and they have three children: Andrew, Becky and Emma Jane.

CHRIS SINKINSON is a lecturer in Old Testament and Apologetics at Moorlands College in the south of England. He has degrees in English and Philosophy, Biblical Studies and Theology. He has been involved in Christian ministry with the Universities and Colleges Christian Fellowship (UCCF) and in pastoral ministry. Through his teaching he has taken part in archaeological excavations in the Holy

Land, where he also leads student tours. Chris writes a monthly column for *Evangelicals Now* and has written a number of books including *Confident Christianity*, published by IVP in 2012. He is married to Ros and together they bring up two young boys and a West Highland terrier!

HEATHER TOMLINSON is a former business journalist on *The Independent on Sunday* and the *Guardian*, and more recently has written for the evangelical publication *Christianity*. She has also worked for several years in the NHS in various roles within mental health, latterly as a trainee clinical psychologist. She lives in Lincolnshire and works as a freelance writer and journalist. You can contact her on Twitter at @HeatherTomli.

RAVI ZACHARIAS was born in Madras, India in 1946 and grew up in a nominally Anglican household. He was an atheist until the age of seventeen, when he tried to commit suicide. While he was in hospital, a local Christian worker brought him a Bible and told his mother to read to him from John 14. Ravi says that it was John 14:19 that led him to commit his life to Christ. After moving to Canada and studying in the United States, he was ordained by the Christian and Missionary Alliance and commissioned as an international evangelist. He founded *Ravi Zacharias International Ministries* in 1984. He has written numerous books, including *A Shattered Visage: The Real Face of Atheism; Can Man Live Without God;* and *The Grand Weaver*. He and his wife Margie have three grown children – Sarah, Naomi and Nathan.

1

A BIOLOGIST
explains why he is not an Atheist

DONALD BRUCE

APPROACHING THE QUESTION

I am a scientist and I think like one. That is one of the main reasons that I am not an atheist.

As a mid-teenager who had a passion for chemistry, I began to ask myself the big questions about life, like

who am I?
what shall I do?
what's the meaning of life?
what happens when you die?

I decided I should seek answers in the way a scientist would. I reasoned that a scientist would look for evidence, as objectively as he could; he would try to follow reasoned argument, and follow the implications through to their logical conclusions. He would not have favouritism towards any preferred option. His conclusion would be the one to which he was led by the evidence. This would be how a scientist would do it, and so I would try to do the same.

As a result, several years later, I committed my life to Jesus Christ, and invited Him to be, as we say, my Saviour, my Lord and my God. I considered that the accumulating evidence pointed to this as the obvious choice. To do anything else would fail the conditions I had set myself. It was still a step of faith, as indeed it is to be an atheist. But it was faith which rested on substance that had stood up to serious scrutiny as far as I was concerned.

Setting it out like that might sound as if it was a carefully focused research project. In reality it was a much more haphazard process over some four to five years, while I studied chemistry (and a lot of other subjects), trained hard as a promising young athlete, discovered a wider world of culture, society and the arts, and much else.

But looking back, there were definite threads running through, and some key points where I drew a conclusion, upon which the next phase of my search then built. Gradually a picture emerged which came into focus around the person of Jesus Christ in the Christian Gospels – who He was and whether, as was claimed, He was God in human form, dying to win spiritual salvation and rising beyond death to offer eternal life to all who would receive Him.

My chapter in this book seeks to explain some of the key threads and factors which led me to the conclusion that this was truth with a capital T – not merely what I decided to believe, but Truth in the sense that it was true objectively, 'out there', whether I chose to believe it or not.

THE PHILOSOPHICAL CASE:
ORDER, RATIONALITY, CONSCIOUSNESS AND EXISTENCE

The first question was how to explain how everything that exists comes to be. In our experience, things do not simply come out of nothing. So what did all that we see around us come out of? And why is it so ordered, consistent and rational, and why do human beings have the capacity to understand it?

One possibility is the philosophical idea that 'it', the universe, has always just been there. This underlies the notion of monistic religions of the east, but to me it ran into scientific problems that to keep going, the universe requires a source of energy or some form of spontaneous creation. The Steady State theory, which proposed this, was not supported by the data. The evidence pointed towards the Big Bang theory. But what caused the Bang? If there was an initiating 'singularity' of unbelievably dense matter which exploded into the Big Bang, why did this singularity exist in the first place?

There are currently several cosmological theories of what, if anything, preceded this state. It is also not clear whether we have any way of knowing. Physicist Stephen Hawking's much-publicized claim that fluctuations in a quantum vacuum did not need anyone (God) to 'light the blue touch paper' has been extensively refuted, largely because it misses the point. What he described is not what we think of when we say 'vacuum' – a space with nothing in it at all. What he describes is a very rich vacuum, a space with physical properties pregnant for something to happen into. But why did such an initial state exist at all? Indeed why do the equations and laws of physics exist without a universe for them to describe?[1] We end up with what existentialist philosopher Jean-Paul Sartre called the ultimate philosophical question: why does anything exist rather than nothing?

Here science is silent, because with questions such as this – and indeed most of the really important questions humans ask about life and its meaning – it has no voice. They lie outside science's proper field of competence. Whether we like it or not, we have entered the arena of philosophy and theology. At this point, every human person makes what are philosophical and theological judgments and decisions. It is part of being human. Although few people are philosophers or articulate easily in the language of philosophical theology, everyone at this point has a view they hold about the world – a philosophy – whether it is only dimly perceived or something they have carefully thought through. I did try to think this through and my answer was that there had to be God. Why?

Oxford philosopher Keith Ward wrote a brilliant and witty book, *Why There Almost Certainly Is a God*, in response to Richard Dawkins's *The God Delusion*. Early in his argument he makes an important point. Any attempt to explain what we see around

---

1   John C. Lennox, *God and Stephen Hawking* (Oxford: Lion Hudson, 2010).

us in purely material terms – just stuff – has to explain how and why consciousness and mind come to exist. Dawkins argues that these are merely unplanned aspects which emerge (late) in a blind process of evolution from purely material origin. Ward challenges this at a number of different levels.[2]

He argues that materialism is not simple and does not provide a sufficient explanation for mind and consciousness. Amid a 'zoo of flickering insubstantial virtual wave-particles' the very nature of material substance is uncertain, mysterious but highly complex. No one knows what consciousness really is. The materialist's case is not there. But he also points out that most of the great classical philosophers from the Greeks onwards 'argued that the ultimate reality, often hidden under the appearance of the material world of time and space, is mind or Spirit.'

Ward argues that mind and consciousness have always existed outside time and space in God, who has designed a universe such that beings would in due course evolve with their own finite version of consciousness. He maintains that this is not only perfectly reasonable but is a far more satisfactory explanation. That to me is the scientist's search – what explanation best fits the data which I have: the universe and its order, human beings and what they are like, myself and my consciousness.

The materialist claim to explain away God as an entirely unnecessary add-on to a material universe fudges an important question about how we explain things. While you can scan my brain for signals, if you want to find out what I am actually thinking about, you have to ask me. This involves a different, and equally valid, sort of knowledge from scientific data. This is personal knowledge. Most of the time we explain what people do, not in terms of synapses and electricity, but in terms of intentions, desires, enjoyment, aspirations, and so on.

As brain scientist Donald MacKay observed many years ago, personal and scientific accounts are complementary descriptions,

---

2   Keith Ward, *Why There Almost Certainly Is a God* (Oxford: Lion Hudson, 2008), pp. 12-14.

each operating at a different level.[3] When some scientists allege that something is 'nothing but' molecules, genes, memes, synapses or whatever, they make a very basic philosophical mistake. It is known technically as ontological reductionism, which MacKay simply called 'nothing-buttery'. Personal knowledge is not reducible to scientific knowledge in any plausible way, nor is belief in God.

Imagine two people walking along a cliff top. Out at sea, suddenly a bright red flare shoots across the sky. One of them is a physicist who gets out her camera and films the event, and from her GPS location is able to calculate the trajectory and velocity of the flare, the wavelength of the light, and so on. She goes back and writes up a concise description of what she observed. The other is a scout, who says, 'That's a distress flare; I must run and tell the coastguard!' Both of them gave an accurate and valid description of what they saw. But they were different, and complementary, with different aims in mind. The scientific account addressed 'how?'; the relational, common-sense account answered 'why?'. There can be complementary ways of looking at the world, each telling different sorts of stories.[4]

IS REALITY PERSONAL OR IMPERSONAL?

Ward, MacKay and others put all this much better. To my youthful logic, it simply did not make sense to me that I am a person who thinks he has some significance in a universe that either had no purpose or a cause that was purely impersonal.

From a long-standing interest in astronomy, I had a sense of the vastness and utter impersonality of the universe. I reasoned that everything about me that I am, all I had ever done or might do in life, everything I felt, enjoyed, feared, hoped, every relationship I ever had, anything to which I attach meaning – all these were utterly insignificant in the cosmos. My life, encompassing a few dozen revolutions of an 8,000 mile-diameter ball of rock round a smaller-than-average star with a finite lifetime, could be neglected

---

3   Donald MacKay, *The Clockwork Image* (Leicester: IVP, 1974).

4   Illustration from Ernest Lucas, *Genesis Today* (London: Scripture Union, 1989), pp. 7-8.

entirely in the grand sweep of impersonal forces, matter, space and time. Nothing would even register that I had existed. This simply did not make sense. Indeed, if a materialistic account is all that there is, then it could be argued that humans are the least adapted beings which are known to have evolved in the universe. We believe we have meaningful relationships, something called love, but in cold reality these are all purely relative, transient illusions with no absolute value at all. We believe in design and purpose for our lives in an undesigned universe. If evolutionary processes have blindly led to the emergence of beings who *think* they have significance, in a universe where nothing is more than physics, chemistry and biology, then we are profoundly out of kilter with reality. Alternatively, this purely materialistic account is simply inadequate to describe reality.

To me, the proposition that there is a real, infinite yet personal, God makes far more sense as an explanation than an utterly purposeless, utterly cold, impersonal, monochrome alternative, which does not make sense of reality. As my wife Ann said when she became a Christian, 'it's like seeing life in colour for the first time.' This then is one of the fundamental reasons why I am not an atheist. Christian belief is true because it makes sense of reality in a way the major alternatives do not.

Truth You Can Lean On

Christianity also coheres with another sense of truth: truth as something you can lean on and it doesn't fall over under the pressure. It works. It is possible to attempt to live according to the teachings of Jesus Christ about God, life, morals, and so on. I often fail but it is because of failings in me, not in His teaching. Materialism does not work because people do not live in practice as if they and all other people were merely material stuff.

I was once asked to chair a talk by a prominent atheist about the purpose of science being to free us from superstitions. Afterwards I challenged him as to why he, as a fellow chemist, attached such high purpose to science if, in his view, the universe is merely material and has no purpose. His reply was, 'One must have lesser purposes.' This seemed to me a cop-out, which undermined the philosophy he had been advocating, because he could not live with the cold logic of his own presuppositions. I would suggest that a human being cannot live consistently as though nothing has any meaning.

Twenty-first-century Britain is highly sceptical of truth claims, that there is anything that does not fall over. And it is quite right to do this – except for God. Nothing else is either big enough or consistent enough to uphold the trust that anyone would put in it, if you were to build a life on it. No human idea, goal, person, relationship, institution or aspiration can bear the weight. It was not intended to. It is sad, but not entirely surprising, that newspapers and historians spend so much time debunking heroes that they or their predecessors had built up, sometimes only a short time before.

HUMAN NATURE

The failure of our heroes brings me to my third piece of evidence for which I sought an answer. What gives the most realistic understanding of the way human beings are, the way I am, the way people behave in relationship to others and in societies and communities?

On the one hand, humans are capable both of the most extraordinary creativity, brilliance and insight, of generosity and love, and, on the other hand, of the most awful violence and destruction, of each other and nature, and such selfish disregard for others.

Again, at this crucial point, the fundamental insights of Christian teaching make sense: that humans are made in God's image but that that image is spoilt by our own self-will and actions.

It is because human beings reflect in some measure the attributes and characteristics of God that they are capable of the most wonderful creativity, insight, ingenuity and love. Science itself springs from the God-given mandate to explore all creation and understand it, and technology from the irrepressible curiosity and ingenuity God has set within humans. But our nature is that of an image, reflecting something else, not an independent form which came into being all by itself and existing in its own right. When we try to make the image self-standing, as though it had no original from which it came, the picture becomes marred.

Human beings are not God. It is when we try to do without God, or pretend to be gods in our own right, that we most fall into uncharacteristic behaviour. According to the biblical accounts, this is what lies at the root both of the horrible distortions of humans behaving badly, of which history, ancient and modern, is full, and also of the more ordinary failings of my own character and that of everyone I know. The fact that we choose to do so is out of kilter with our very nature. It has made, within each human being, a part that has gone rotten inside, which spoils the otherwise beautiful taste of a person's life and achievement and relationships.

If we are nothing but stuff – cells, genes, molecules and whatever – why have we got this split personality? Indeed, why do we recognize one as laudable, good and thrilling and the other as ghastly and deplorable? In a materialistic model, our behaviour is just what we do. Our values of good and bad are just human social impositions on a natural order that has no ultimate morality.

Materialism does not adequately explain our humanity, whereas the Christian understanding makes sense. It also helps to explain something else important, which I have only come to see later, after many years as a Christian.

The failure of Christians, individually and as the church, to live out what we believe strikes many as an inconsistency which seriously detracts from what we claim as truth. The Christian understanding of our humanity in no way excuses this, but it explains why it is the case. The pervasiveness of what it calls 'sin' runs so deep that, as much as we begin to change our lives for the better, the poisoned vein remains until we die, because only a complete remake will finally extract it.

For each Christian, eternal life has begun, but it remains 'a work in progress'. He or she will still show a mixture of good and bad behaviour. Christians acting collectively as the church will do the same. The church was meant for service, not for power, and has usually made a mess when it uses power, because we believers are not 'redeemed' enough to handle power properly. Awful things have been done, which though said to be 'in God's name' were in reality done in the name of our unredeemed nature, not in the name of Jesus Christ.

He taught that it is only after death, in resurrection, that the poison is finally drained out, and we will experience the life in full harmony with God and each other – the kingdom of God. For this lifetime, we have forgiveness and at least a start to work out something of that kingdom on earth, but its fulfilment remains in the final resurrection, when Jesus returns for good.

THE OTHER SIDE OF THE COIN: GOD'S EVIDENCE

What I have presented so far are mostly conclusions about the evidence from one side of the picture, drawing on my observations from nature, from myself and from fellow humans – what some early scientists called the book of God's works, and what some theologians call natural theology. These things point me to belief in God who is both the infinite, transcendent Creator, and also is personal – who is Himself a person and to whom I can, at least in some way, relate personally.

This line of investigation could take me this far, but not much further.[5] To know more would require that this God had communicated to me in some form – what theologians call revelation. The Christian claim is that God has indeed communicated – in verbal form in the pages of what we call the Bible, but supremely in the best way that God could show: by becoming a human being Himself in the person of Jesus Christ.

This is what makes the Christian claim surpass that of all religions. It is either outrageous or true. Investigating this claim is the other side of the picture, and I have already begun to draw on it, in a biblical understanding of being human.

The first question is: why Jesus and why then?

---

5   Francis Schaeffer, *The God Who Is There* (London: Hodder & Stoughton, 1968), ch. 5 (How do we know it is true?).

One might speculate theoretically about all the various ways such a divine Being could choose to make Himself known to humans.[6] But it is not unreasonable that the ultimate reality of the universe became a human being at a particular point in space and time, to reveal Himself to humanity, and demonstrated the fact in numerous ways, but most of all in rising from the dead, as no other person has.

Others in this volume explore the person of Jesus Christ, His life, teachings and miracles, more fully. I will focus on the central claims – that He died for all human sin, that He rose from the dead to offer eternal life for all who would believe, and that the essential details have been recorded for everyone thereafter to examine for themselves.

The claim is that the authors of the Gospels were eyewitnesses or had spoken to eyewitnesses of the resurrection. To me, the very style of the accounts, their similarities and differences, had the feel of what eyewitnesses say, rather than something you would have made up. Our postmodern twenty-first century is dubious about putting such reliance on ancient documents, but it was significant to me that far more manuscripts are available, and far closer to the originals, than almost any other document of the Roman world. But above all it is the *content* of accounts that demanded serious explanation.

That Jesus of Nazareth died by crucifixion outside Jerusalem in about A.D. 30 is reasonably well accepted. The circumstances under which He died, when He might so easily have got off, are intriguing in themselves. The authors clearly viewed Him as something quite different from a misguided religious zealot or revolutionary. But the key evidence that He rose from the dead, quite simply defies any other reasonable explanation of the available data. Had any of the various alternative explanations been true, the resurrection story would not have lasted more than a few days or weeks. If it

---

6   I use the pronoun 'he' recognizably as an approximation, because no pronoun or other common form of words in English can convey an equal balance of gender and the concept of God that both embraces genderedness as we experience it and simultaneously transcends it.

was deception or a made-up story, someone would have produced the body or blown the gaff.

To have invented it, when they had the body all the time, does not square with the consequences which followed in the lives of the believers. The reactions of the Greek philosophical elite in Athens suggest that people were not more gullible towards the idea of someone rising from the dead in those days (Acts 17:16-34). To follow this Man and be a member of this emerging sect rapidly became something very serious indeed. The thing became a head-on conflict, first with the Jewish ruling religious councils and then the imperial authorities. If you knew you had made it up, you just wouldn't do that.

In the film *Shallow Grave*, the collapse of the friends' conspiracy, in hiding the body they found in an Edinburgh flat, is all too typically human. If the disciples of Jesus were just deluded and believed that a resurrection had happened, then where *was* the body all the time, and why did no one produce it to refute the whole thing before it 'went viral'?

To have made it all up also doesn't fit with a change from a small, scared band of people into a movement which eventually superseded the Roman empire. It is a change that has gone on happening in millions of people who have continued to encounter the risen Christ, in countless other times and places and circumstances, down to the present day. We too have found the ancient accounts to have the ring of truth.

REASONS BEYOND JUST REASON

The Christian message as presented to me when I was about nineteen also gave me an answer to a long-standing question. Whereas I would not have called myself a particularly 'bad' person, I knew full well that if there is a God, who was holy and had laws and commandments and things, I did not meet His standards. Trying to be religious did not seem a very realistic option, based on any attempts of mine so far. But what the Christian gospel turned out to be was not what I was expecting, and it was absolutely liberating.

My conclusion – that I could never be good enough for God – was in fact quite correct. In holiness terms, the high-jump bar was set so high that I'd never get over even by trying to pole-vault it. But Jesus Christ had cleared it for me. Based on His death for me, in my place, I was now offered absolute forgiveness for all time – past, present and future – as an act of grace. All I had to do was accept it, on faith, and start to try to live it out.

This total acceptance of a human being by the Almighty God was indeed very good news, because it is not about my ability to keep a set of standards in order to achieve sufficient goodness to 'get in'.

I must also add that the lives of those in a small Christian group I had come into contact with impressed me with their genuine concern and caring for me personally, in a way that stood out. Of itself, this does not prove that what they believed was true, but it was entirely consistent with what was supposed to happen, according to what it said on the tin. And there was an indefinable sense of attraction to something warm and inviting about God's invitation to me, a sort of homecoming, without my having had a very overtly Christian upbringing, to the point that eventually I wanted to become a Christian.

Ah, but was this a case of God as just a projection of my desires, or to allay my feelings of insignificance, as Feuerbach alleged in the nineteenth century? That sounds a plausible argument on the face of it – until you realize that Feuerbach had already made a prior assumption that God does *not* exist. He was in fact using a circular argument which proves nothing at all. If you assume God doesn't exist then you might talk about projections.

But if God does exist, then it is entirely reasonable that God has implanted a desire for Him inside each one of us. The real question is not about projections, but whether God actually exists.

However, it has an interesting sting in the tail. If God doesn't exist, why project if there is actually nothing there? In an impersonal godless universe, that people should come up with the idea of God does not make sense. Is it not more likely that there indeed is a God and that we have a desire for God imprinted upon us? The God-explanation coheres better than a false projection.

Strangely, the same holds for the question of suffering, which for many is a real stumbling block to belief in God. My time-bound, earth-bound perspective is too small for me to demand that God explain Himself on my terms, before I will accept Him.

However, it also occurs to me that if the material universe is all that there is, why call something suffering? It's just 'what happens', merely 'what is'. There is pain, but in an ultimately utterly impersonal universe, so what? The concept of suffering implies some other, better state with which we compare it, one without the suffering. It implies that somewhere there should be a musical resolution of the horrible jarring note of human pain. If not, suffering is actually a meaningless idea. It only means something if there is good somewhere, a final resolution.

Rather than being a fist raised at God, I suggest that it is a cry for God. For only God could provide the solution. And the Christian claim is that in the mystery of the death of Jesus Christ on the cross and His rising from the dead, God has done so. From what I have experienced of God, I can accept on faith that there can be a final explanation for suffering and that it is somehow bound up in the cross of Jesus, where God took the entire pain of human suffering on to Himself to release us from it.

THE EVIDENCE OF EXPERIENCE

This brings me to my final piece of evidence: the vast cumulative evidence I now have –

- from attempting to put into practice the assumption that there is a personal almighty God, rather than nothing, who relates to me in the way the Bible says He does

- from treating the Bible as God's propositional and practical communication with me

- from praying and expecting answers

- and from seeking God's power and love and less selfishness to change my life, and so on.

In doing this, I sense that there really is something 'there'. At different times it might be a sense of a presence, or exultation, or peace or not peace, of being in Wesley's words 'strangely warmed'. It is as if I really do have a relationship with God as my heavenly Father, a sense of the person of Jesus Christ being real to me, not merely historical, and the Holy Spirit as a presence – guiding, restraining and prompting me.

If I were now to have to provide an alternative explanation for all the innumerable events that have occupied this relationship of some forty-four years, it would not cohere with reality. I would feel indeed that I would be deliberately trying to find reasons not to believe, rather than being true to the evidence. My best explanation is that God really is there in Jesus Christ.

CONCLUSION

I set out to find what gives the best explanation of the universe I saw around me, of people, of society and of myself. There is a lot of other exploration and evidence that I have not had space to include. But I concluded that there had to be God –

- not a quasi-human god of ancient Greece or Babylon, of limited powers, capricious nature and doubtful morals

- nor yet the impersonal pan-everything concept of ultimate reality of monist religions

- not merely a remote first cause who set the clockwork mechanism going and left it to its own devices.

God had to be infinite in power and knowledge but also personal; God must be transcendent but also immanent to me. The Being whom Jesus of Nazareth called 'your heavenly Father' (e.g. Matt. 6:26) seemed to be just that Being.

This leads us to the ultimate issue about why someone is or is not an atheist. It becomes a matter of will, because a Being greater than I becomes the focus of the question.

At some point in my search I came to a discovery. For all our amazing capabilities, humans are ultimately dependent beings, not independent ones. I was not merely considering whether or not to assent to a set of propositions. I was confronted with an act of will on my part to accept the invitation of the God who really is there if, as it increasingly seemed to me, the propositions did have the ring of truth about them.

What began as a search for the meaning of life, if any, became a challenge to bow my knee before this almighty divine Being, and come into a relationship of obedience and trust with God, through Jesus Christ.

The atheist has faith too, and it too is really a matter of the will. In the end, is a person prepared willingly to bow the knee to God and His welcome or cling to the illusion of independent autonomy?

God can do without me. Yet He wants to do *with* me. He invites me to come, to come close – as close as I dare. As a scientist seeking to be true to the evidence, I have done so, and I have not regretted it.

2

A UNIVERSITY CHAPLAIN
explains why he is not an Atheist

ALISTAIR DONALD

There are many reasons why I am not an atheist, but one in particular has been a prominent strand in my own life: the firm belief that the natural world points very clearly to the existence of an all-powerful and all-wise Creator. This, of course, goes against the grain of much thinking today, when it is often believed that science has proved matters to be otherwise. The universe and all life on earth are instead widely held to be solely the product of blind and purposeless processes. Science and religion are considered to be – wrongly as I hope to show – in fundamental conflict and have been for hundreds of years.

With my background in environmental research and policy work, and my current work as chaplain in a university specializing in science and technology, I am well aware that this is a live issue for many people today. Religious faith is seen by some as a harmless illusion, and by an outspoken few as a dangerous delusion. But in either case faith seems to bear no relation to what is real, since science is thought to have been the victor in a science-religion war.

This view spills over beyond science to the media and to the ideas that many people have about morality. So a journalist who knows next to nothing about science can gaily write that morality is what you make it, since human beings are merely 'dancing to the music of their DNA'. Such thinking bolsters sceptics in their scepticism, and causes Christians to worry that their faith might be hanging on a loose nail.

There are, of course, many individual scientists who are Christians or who at any rate believe in God, but these are not the ones we usually hear about. Instead, those who front the fabulously filmed TV documentaries on astronomy or wildlife are usually atheists, often parading their unbelief in a way that would be unacceptable for believing scientists to do with their religious belief. In this climate, to call into question even the wildest atheist speculations about the origin of the universe or the origin of life is to risk being written off as 'attacking science' or 'trying to smuggle religion into science'.

I have puzzled and reflected over the relationship of science and faith for some decades now. I remember sitting in a first-year biology class at university in the mid-1970s, when the lecturer paused and said, 'Avoid teleology, because it makes bad science.' Being a fairly normal eighteen-year-old, I hadn't a clue what that word meant. But I did go and look it up in a dictionary afterwards, and I remember being very puzzled when I found that it referred to purpose and design. For the lecturer was known to be an evangelical Christian, a deacon in the local Baptist Church, and his warning to the class about teleology struck me as very odd: why on earth would a Christian want to deny purpose and design?

The more I have read and reflected on this issue, the odder that warning has seemed. For, as we shall see below, there are good reasons to think that a design framework is not the 'science-stopper' often claimed (saying 'God made it' allegedly prevents you from being curious about nature). In fact, a design framework has much to commend it in moving the scientific project forward, quite apart from its value in suggesting persuasively that the natural world points beyond itself to a Mind behind matter, a Creator of all things.

In the rest of this chapter, I will look in turn at three areas where science and religion have often been held to be in conflict: the scope of science, the history of science and finally some findings of science, particularly from the stars (cosmology) and the cell (biology). In each case, I hope that sceptical readers and believing readers will each be given food for thought – challenging or encouraging as the case may be.

The Scope of Science

It may be a surprise to learn that there is no single agreed definition of what science is among philosophers of science. Long ago Augustine said that everybody knows what time is until they try to define it, and it's a similar situation with science. Certain elements do certainly crop up: hypotheses, experiment, data, evidence, modification of hypotheses, and so on. But a hard definition is surprisingly difficult. We should remember this when someone says this or that activity is 'simply not science'.

Michael Ruse, a philosopher of biology, has tried this definition: 'Science by definition deals only with the natural, the repeatable, that which is governed by law.'[1] Now that sounds plausible enough, until we notice that his definition rules out cosmology and the origin and history of life. You cannot repeat those events, and mainstream cosmology cheerfully admits that the laws of physics do not apply in the first moments after the Big Bang. So Ruse's definition rather loses its shine.

Science derives much of its impressive cultural authority in our society from the galaxy of new technology and gadgets that we all enjoy. We can travel to the other side of the world in a metal tube with wings, confident that we will reach our destination safely. We can send and receive messages and pictures in our personal communicators way beyond what was mere fantasy in *Star Trek* just a generation ago. And we also benefit from the development of new drugs and other medical treatment, and so on.

If we were only dealing with these branches of science, then we might be happy to go along with the late Stephen Jay Gould's famous model of the relations between science and religion of 'Non-Overlapping Magisteria' (NOMA). It even sounds quite

---

1   M. Ruse, 'Will science ever fail?' in *New Scientist*, 8 August 1992, pp. 32-5.

respectful, by recognizing religion as a valid field of study, albeit totally segregated from science. As an old hymn said: 'You in your small corner and I in mine.'[2]

But for some branches of science, this really won't do. When we're dealing with matters such as the origin of the universe, the origin of life, the phenomenon of consciousness and brain science, and so on, matters are very different. Philosophy – usually materialist philosophy (the view that matter and energy are all that exists, that the spiritual realm is purely imaginary) – can easily be smuggled into science. This then becomes not science, but 'scientism', the belief that science is the only source of all true knowledge.

Here are some examples. When the late Carl Sagan introduced his TV series, 'Cosmos', by saying, 'The cosmos is all that is or was or ever will be', that was a statement of his atheist belief, not a conclusion of his astronomical studies. And when palaeontologist George Gaylord Simpson wrote: 'Man is the result of a purposeless, natural process that did not have him in mind',[3] he did not reach that view from his painstaking study of fossils. Harvard geneticist Richard Lewontin rather gave the game away when he wrote that it was not that the methods and institutions of science compel us to accept a materialistic explanation of the natural world, but rather that this arises from a prior commitment to exclusively materialistic causes – 'for we cannot allow a Divine foot in the door'.[4]

Some of the most intelligent people cannot see that science, for all its wonderful insights, cannot give a total view of all truth and cannot disprove the existence of God.

One of the world's most famous and brilliant scientists is theoretical physicist Stephen Hawking. His first best-seller, the slim volume *A Brief History of Time*, adorned many bookshelves (but was perhaps not taken down and read as often as the author might

2   Hymn *Jesus bids us shine* by Susan Warner (1819-85).

3   G. G. Simpson, *The Meaning of Evolution* (New Haven, Yale University Press, revised edition 1967), p. 345.

4   R. Lewontin, *Billions and billions of demons* in New York Review of Books, 1997 (review of Carl Sagan's 1997 book *The Demon-Haunted World: Science as a Candle in the Dark* [Random House]).

have liked!). At the end of that book, Hawking looked forward to there being a 'Theory of Everything', at which point he said we would '... know the Mind of God'.

But in 2010 he changed his tune, to worldwide headlines such as, 'Stephen Hawking Says Physics Leaves No Room for God.' His newer, co-authored book was called *The Grand Design*,[5] and it now seems quite clear that Hawking 'doesn't do God'. So what has changed? Well, it's not the science, strangely enough. As Professor John Lennox of Oxford has pointed out[6], what has changed is that Hawking has ventured outside his field to philosophy. Strange to say, he does so quite unwittingly. He first lists the traditional Big Questions such as, 'How can we understand the world?', 'Where did all this come from?' and 'Did the universe need a Creator?' He then argues that these questions, the traditional concerns of metaphysics, are now to be answered by science, since 'philosophy is dead'.[7]

Can you see the problem here? His claim that 'philosophy is dead' is itself a statement of philosophy! And so his claim must be false. Moreover, Hawking's case is that the laws of physics, not the will of God, give the real explanation of how the universe came into being. He argues that the Big Bang (the origin of the universe) was the inevitable consequence of these laws: 'Because there is a law such as gravity, the universe can and will create itself out of nothing.'[8]

But what Hawking is doing here is confusing law with something else, usually called agency. The laws of mathematics may be true, but they never placed a pound in my pocket! And while Newton's laws of motion may explain the movement of billiard balls on the pool table, it's the player with the crack aim who pots the ball, not the laws themselves. In the same way, laws such as gravity cannot by themselves create anything.

---

5   S. Hawking and L. Mlodinow, *The Grand Design* (London: Bantam Press, 2010).

6   J. Lennox, *God and Stephen Hawking: Whose design is it anyway?* (London: Lion Hudson, 2011).

7   Hawking and Mlodinow, op. cit., p. 5.

8   Ibid., p. 180.

WHY I AM NOT AN ATHEIST

The conflict usually portrayed as one between science and faith is in fact another conflict altogether. It is a clash between two opposing world views, two opposing faiths:

- the belief that there is a God, and that therefore Mind came before matter;

- and the belief that matter is all there is, and that therefore mind is merely a product of matter and God is purely imaginary.

We will look below at which of these two beliefs best fits with some important recent scientific evidence, and the answer may come as quite a surprise.

But first we need to turn to another important area which has been seen as a key battleground between science and religion.

THE HISTORY OF SCIENCE

Most of us are used to the idea that there has been a fundamental conflict between science and religion during the last few hundred years of Western science. The trial and imprisonment of Galileo is often brought forward as a prime exhibit in making this case. But among historians of science, it is very widely accepted today that, far from there being a conflict, there was in fact a close harmony. Witnesses in support of this view make up a veritable *Who's Who* of scientific discovery: Copernicus, Galileo (yes, Galileo – see below), Kepler, Pascal, Boyle, Newton, Faraday, Babbage, Mendel, Pasteur, Kelvin and Clerk Maxwell.

These were all theists, and most were, in fact, practicing Christians. And it wasn't just that these luminaries happened to live at a time when a religious outlook was culturally respectable and indeed the majority view in society. As is clear from their writings, it was their own faith in a Creator that drove them to make discoveries about the works of the One they believed in. A pithy summing up of this view comes from C. S. Lewis, who said: 'Men became scientific because they expected law in nature, and they expected law in nature because they believed in a Legislator.'[9]

This is why it is so outrageous when secular revisionists say that religious faith is a 'science-stopper'. History shows that it's quite

---

9   C. S. Lewis, *Miracles* (London: Collins, 1947), p. 110.

the opposite – it's a science-motivator. No wonder, then, that James Clerk Maxwell, the first Director of the Cavendish Laboratory in Cambridge – workplace over the years of no fewer than 29 Nobel prize-winners in Physics – had this inscription from Psalm 111:2 carved over its doors as a motto: 'Great are the works of the Lord; they are pondered by all who delight in them.'

So how then did the 'conflict thesis' gain acceptance? And how does it live on in the work of influential popular commentators even as it is rejected by historians of science? The 'conflict thesis' can be traced to the influence of two Victorian books: J. W. Draper's *History of the Conflict between Religion and Science*, published in 1875, and A. D. White's *A History of the Warfare of Science with Theology in Christendom* from twenty years later.[10] Both books were part of a movement designed to discredit the church (especially the established Church of England) and to replace it with what Thomas Huxley called 'the church scientific'. Scientists were, in the words of Francis Galton, to be termed its 'scientific priesthood'.

The books by Draper and White continue to this day to have an enormous impact, either directly or indirectly through the influence of Bertrand Russell, who adopted their arguments with gusto in his *A History of Western Philosophy*. They view the entire history of Western science through the prism of a conflict. Where there was no evidence to support the thesis, White merely made it up.

A case in point is the religious opposition that James Simpson allegedly faced in Edinburgh when he used anaesthesia to relieve the pain of childbirth, which he did from 1847. White thunders as follows: 'From pulpit after pulpit Simpson's use of chloroform was denounced as impious and contrary to Holy Writ; texts were cited abundantly, the ordinary declaration being that to use chloroform was "to avoid one part of the primeval curse on women".'[11] This is

---

10   See further P. J. Sampson, *6 Modern Myths about Christianity and Western Civilization* (Downers Grove, IL: InterVarsity Press, 2001), especially chapters 1, 2 and 5.

11   A. D. White, *A History of the Warfare of Science with Theology in Christendom* (London: Macmillan, 1896) Vol II, p. 63.

fearsome stuff! But detailed investigation of both the medical and religious literature of the day has shown that religious opposition to Simpson's use of anaesthesia in childbirth was virtually non-existent. Such opposition as did exist was, more prosaically, on medical or physiological grounds.

A second example involves the use of entirely spurious quotations. Regarding the impact of the theory of Copernicus that the earth rotated round the sun rather than *vice versa*, Bertrand Russell attributes this direct quotation to Calvin: 'Who will venture to place the authority of Copernicus above that of the Holy Spirit?'[12] Significantly, Russell doesn't give a reference for this. But Thomas Kuhn, in his 1957 book *The Copernican Revolution,* attributes the Calvin quotation to White, and adds for good measure that the quotation can be traced to Calvin's commentary on Genesis. But Calvin makes no mention of Copernicus in that commentary, or indeed anywhere else. Recent debate tends to the view that the quotation was simply invented in the late nineteenth century to bolster the somewhat threadbare case for the conflict thesis.

As previously mentioned, that case has as its centre Galileo, to whom we must now return. No one today would want to defend the Roman Catholic Church's treatment of Galileo. Indeed even the Church itself wouldn't now wish to do so, given its apology over the matter in 1992. But the way Galileo is often used as a poster-boy for atheism and materialism in making a case that science and religion are always at odds is really quite absurd. He believed in Scripture before he started his campaign, and he believed it when he finished.

In popularizing the theory of Copernicus, who had died largely unopposed more than twenty years before Galileo's birth, Galileo was initially attacked by philosophers before his little difficulty with the Pope. And he was attacked because he dared to question, on the basis of careful observations through his telescope, the reigning scientific theory, the Aristotelian dogma that had ruled for hundreds of years.

---

12   B. Russell, *History of Western Philosophy* (London: Allen & Unwin, 1947), p. 550.

Aristotle had held that the earth was stationary, the various spheres rotating around the earth being seen as in a realm of perfection without blemishes. So when Galileo reported seeing sunspots and other apparent imperfections through his telescope, his observations were seen as a direct challenge to the ruling Aristotelian view, firmly accepted by most philosophers of the day as well as by the church. Yes, Bible texts such as Psalm 93:1 ('The world is firmly established; it cannot be moved') were invoked to bolster Aristotle's view that the earth, not the sun, was at the centre of the solar system. But Galileo's protest was not against the use of Scripture but against what he saw as its misuse in propping up a defunct theory.

Yet it has to be said that Galileo didn't approach the conflict very wisely. We would say today that he was lacking a good PR adviser. For in a publication presenting the two opposing views in the form of a dramatic dialogue, he put the Aristotelian view of his erstwhile friend the Pope in the mouth of one *Simplicitus* – the Fool. He also irritated the scholars by having the effrontery to write in Italian rather than Latin. All these factors are in the mix in this curious tale. So, whatever else may be said, it's certainly not a straight story of science versus religion, and the light of progress versus dark dungeons. Galileo was in fact held under benign house arrest.

So the 'conflict thesis' of the relation between science and religion just doesn't fit the historical reality. No wonder that Professor Colin Russell has put it in such strong terms:

> The common belief that the actual relations between religion and science over the last few centuries have been marked by deep and enduring hostility is not only historically inaccurate, but actually a caricature so grotesque that what needs to be explained is how it could possibly have achieved any degree of respectability.[13]

THE FINDINGS OF SCIENCE

As with the matters discussed above, new findings in science are often paraded as if their discovery somehow invalidates the idea of

---

13   C. Russell, *Beliefs and Values in Science Education* (Buckingham: Open University Press, 1995), p. 125.

a Creator. But again we find that this is not the case. Although the existence of God may not be conclusively proved (or disproved) by looking at the natural world, it is arguable that some key recent findings of science fit far better with a God-centred view of reality than with atheism.

When we turn our telescopes to the stars, current scientific thinking is that the universe had a definite beginning – known as the Big Bang. But until a few decades ago, this was not accepted. Instead, the consensus among cosmologists was that the universe had always existed – the Steady State theory. When the Big Bang theory was first proposed, it was stoutly resisted – not on grounds of evidence, but because it sounded too like the first verse in the Bible: 'In the beginning, God created the heavens and the earth.'

And so we have Sir Arthur Eddington, writing this in the journal *Nature* in 1931: 'Philosophically, the notion of a beginning of the present order of Nature is repugnant ... I should like to find a genuine loophole.'[14] Even as recently as 1989, the then editor of the same journal, in response to speculation as to what physical conditions might have prevailed before the Big Bang, wrote this: 'The idea of a beginning is thoroughly unacceptable, because it implies an ultimate origin of our world, and gives creationists ample justification for their beliefs.'[15]

But no matter how much it may have seemed philosophically uncongenial to some, the Big Bang has been widely accepted because that is the way the evidence points.

Another interesting aspect of cosmology is the discovery over recent decades of 'cosmic fine-tuning' – the fact that gravity and the other constants of physics are all 'just so', amazingly fine-tuned in their various values. This is what physicist Paul Davies has called the 'Goldilocks Enigma':[16] as with baby bear's porridge,

---

14   A. Eddington, 'The End of the World: from the Standpoint of Mathematical Physics', in *Nature* 127 (1931), p. 450.

15   J. Maddox, 'Down with the Big Bang', in *Nature* 340 (1989), p. 425.

16   P. Davies, *The Goldilocks Enigma* (London: Penguin, 2007).

the fundamental forces in the observable universe are 'just right' for carbon-based life. Why should this be? Those who argue against the obvious pointer to design (and hence a Designer) in these findings propose that there are multiple universes, with our observable universe just happening to look finely tuned.

That, of course, would not in itself logically remove the need for a Creator. But might the 'multiverse hypothesis' not simply be another case of queasiness in the face of evidence that is philosophically uncongenial? Professor John Polkinghorne is clear that the simpler explanation of one finely tuned universe is to be preferred. After all, surely science is about explaining what we can observe, rather than postulating what in principle we can't observe.

This evidence for a cosmic beginning and for fine-tuning is pretty overwhelming.

Design and DNA

When we turn our attention from telescopes to microscopes, from the stars to the cell, again there seems to be clear evidence of design, although in this case the matter is much more controversial. I mentioned above my puzzlement as a young student as to why a Christian lecturer would want to 'avoid teleology' (i.e. avoid assuming purpose and design in biology). Of course, I soon learned why: because Darwin's theory has rendered design thinking redundant. Or has it? The *impression* of design is certainly clear to all, atheist as well as theist. Hence, Richard Dawkins defines biology as 'the study of complicated things that give the appearance of having been designed for a purpose'.[17] So he stakes all on the deceptiveness of appearances. Francis Crick, co-discoverer of the DNA double helix, says this: 'Biologists must constantly keep in mind that what they see was not designed, but rather evolved.'[18] So apparently a biologist must keep on pinching herself as she looks down the microscope: 'Not designed'!

---

17   R. Dawkins, *The Blind Watchmaker: Why the Evidence of Evolution Reveals a Universe without Design* (London, Longman, 1986), p. 1.

18   F. Crick, *What Mad Pursuit: A Personal View of Scientific Discovery* (New York, Basic Books, 1989), p. 138.

What are we to make of this? Well, of course, in principle the presence of a mechanism does not in itself disprove agency, including divine agency. Knowing about the process of internal combustion does not remove the need for a car engine to have had a designing engineer. And the list of those who are persuaded that random mutation and natural selection are simply the way God did His creating is a distinguished one: Alister McGrath, John Polkinghorne, Denis Alexander and Francis Collins, to name just a few.

Yet there are indications that all is not well with Darwinism as an all-embracing explanation for the development of life. Philosopher of science Thomas Nagel (significantly not a theist, so with no axe to grind on this matter) published a stunning book in 2012 called *Mind and Cosmos*, in which he boldly defends what he terms the 'untutored reaction of incredulity to the reductionist neo-Darwinian account'[19] (i.e. the view that unguided random processes alone account for all life). He writes: 'It is *prima facie* highly implausible that life as we know it is the result of a sequence of physical accidents ...'[20] Anticipating a strong reaction to his book, he adds: 'I realize that such doubts will strike many people as outrageous, but that is because everyone in our secular culture has been browbeaten into regarding the reductive research program as sacrosanct, on the ground that anything else would not be science.'[21]

It is, of course, beyond dispute that natural selection can do certain things very well indeed: modify finch beaks, introduce resistance to antibiotics, and so on. But these are small things. Rather than asking, 'Couldn't God have used this process in creating?' (for those who believe in God, He can, of course, do anything), we can ask a much more interesting scientific question: 'Does random mutation and natural selection actually possess the fabulous creative power usually attributed to it?' For if it does not, then the first question loses its force. Saying we have identified the process

---

19   T. Nagel, *Mind and Cosmos: Why the Materialist Neo-Darwinian Conception of Nature is Almost Certainly False* (Oxford, Oxford University Press, 2012), p. 6.

20   ibid., p. 6.

21   ibid., p. 7.

by which finches acquire thicker beaks over some generations is one thing; saying that the same process *must* therefore account for the origin of birds (with all their organs, feathers, etc) is a quite different claim.

Peering into the nano-world of the living cell, we find mysteries that material explanations alone are struggling to explain. The DNA in our cells – that which makes me me and you you – has been described by Bill Gates (surely the ultimate authority in today's society!) as 'like a computer program, but far, far more advanced than any we've ever created.'

So where did the software that drives the cell come from? Those of us who are parents or grandparents and who have bought computer games for our children have no doubt often wondered why we pay £40 for a flimsy disk. The answer, of course, is that we are paying not just for the physical disk, but for all the hours of work put in by intelligent software engineers. Similarly, the text you are now reading on this page cannot be explained solely by the physics and chemistry of paper and ink; it is held in a matrix of paper and ink, but its origin (for better or worse!) is in the mind of the author. So then, with DNA: must that software really have arisen spontaneously from purposeless, random processes? Is that, in fact, a coherent position? Or does the evidence not instead point to a Mind behind matter? If it takes a human to write a paragraph or even a word, what are we to say about the authorship of the longest word in the universe, the 3-billion-letter word of the human genome?

Former atheist philosopher Antony Flew, who died a few years ago, was certainly persuaded by this evidence to stop being an atheist. No matter how philosophically uncongenial it was to him, when he considered the language-like code that is DNA he felt he had no alternative. Here is how he put it: 'My whole life has been guided by the principle of Plato's Socrates: Follow the evidence, wherever it leads.'[22] Some commentators suggested that Flew had lost his

---

22 Interview with ABC News, *Famous Atheist Now Believes In God*, www.abcnews. go.com/US/wireStory?id=315976.

faculties in the face of approaching death (he was over eighty at the time) – not the kindest of conclusions. But perhaps he was simply doing what he said he was doing: following the evidence where it leads.

THE DEMISE OF 'JUNK DNA'

One of the tests of a robust scientific theory is whether it is good at predicting what has yet to be discovered. Here again, recent discoveries about the living cell have found Darwinian predictions to be wanting, and have instead lent support to the much-despised teleological approach known as 'intelligent design'.

Within the living cell, the proportion of the genome that codes for protein – and therefore has a known use – is very small. In fact, 98 per cent of it has been considered for decades to be useless, and so was dubbed 'Junk DNA'. Time and time again this has been invoked – by atheistic evolutionists and by theistic evolutionists alike – as firm evidence for the process of unguided neo-Darwinism, 'just what we would expect' from long eons of random mutations. As recently as 2006, Francis Collins, the former Director of the Human Genome Project, set this forth very firmly as clear evidence that evolution was the way God had done His creating: otherwise, why would so much junk have been found?

Except that we now know it isn't junk. Literally every week that passes, new scientific papers are being published which reveal whole new levels of function within the living cell in this hitherto ignored genetic material. Far from a design framework being a hindrance to scientific enquiry, it now looks like the hindrance has come from another source – from a remarkable lack of curiosity arising from the mindset that junk is just what would be expected from Darwin's theory. And rather than a design framework being a 'science stopper' or a sign of 'bad science', it is arguable that such an approach would have looked earlier for purpose and function in the parts of DNA that had not yet yielded their secrets.

The type of reasoning outlined above is sometimes dismissed as a 'god-of-the-gaps' argument: when we are confronted with something for which we have no material explanation, we say

God has done it, only to have to retreat ignominiously once our knowledge increases. But the 'god-of-the-gaps' criticism does not apply here, since we are discussing an increase in knowledge rather than a lack. And the *more* we find out about the wonders of the universe and of the living cell, the *more* these things appear to be designed. To adopt such reasoning in cosmology but to exclude it from biology, as many scientists who are also Christians apparently wish to do, seems to me to be both inconsistent and unjustified.

CONCLUSION

Some 3,000 years ago, a young Middle Eastern shepherd was out looking up at the night sky. Perhaps some years later, he wrote a poem about the vivid impression the stars had made on him about God's glory. We have it recorded in the Bible as the first two verses of Psalm 19: 'The heavens declare the glory of God; the skies proclaim the work of his hands. Day after day they pour forth speech; night after night they reveal knowledge.'

After hundreds of years of scientific research, much of it carried out by those who, like Maxwell, shared the Psalmist's faith, what do we find? Far from us having less reason than the Psalmist to believe in God as Creator, we in fact have much, much more – from the stars to the cell. Far from it being proved that 'matter is all there is', there are, in fact, many pointers that Mind came before matter. Far from it being shown that impersonal forces alone caused both the origin and the development of life in all its fabulous diversity, it looks increasingly as if such claims are overblown and neglect the clear evidence of a designing intelligence.

These, then, are some of the reasons why I am not an atheist. There are other reasons, of course, why I am a Christian, but that is another story. For not only does John's Gospel start with, 'In the beginning was the Word'; it also records, 'The Word became flesh, and made his dwelling among us' (John 1:1 and 14).

3

A MISSIONARY
explains why he is not an Atheist

HENK DROST

The most important reason is a strange one: I am not an atheist because of a book. That book is not a normal book like other books.

Of course, any book can have a big influence on one's life. Many people can say that they changed their vision or their behaviour because of a book. But I have experience with an extraordinary book. Through that book Someone started to talk to me. The Bible changed my life.

I was born in a family in Holland. My father was a pastor. My mother was always taking care of her ten children. We went to Papua in Indonesia – at that time a colony of the Netherlands – where my father worked as a missionary. My father travelled so far – and took us with him – to tell other people about God. From my youth I heard the stories of the Bible;

- there are beautiful stories in it;

- there are impressive letters in it;

- there is beautiful poetry in it.

I learned a lot of things from it. But I also learned from other books, of course. What is the difference? The difference is that this book changed my way of thinking and living.

Why? What makes this book special? This book was written by many people from different ages, professions and capabilities. But through all of them God worked so that in this book His plans and thoughts were written. That makes the book the book of God that He uses nowadays to tell us the truth and to change our lives.

How? When I heard as a child the stories from the Bible and later started to read in the Bible, God used His book. God spoke to me. I did not hear a voice but I noticed how the reading of this book had an impact on me. God showed me that He really exists. He showed me who He really is in His infinite power and great love. He also taught me to see who I am.

I remember that I felt more and more uncomfortable when I studied that book. It tells about perfect love – and I missed that. It tells us to live in love – and I didn't. I felt more and more the absence of love in my life. I saw more and more the wrong things that I did. And then I read about the Person who said those beautiful things about love. He not only spoke about love, but also fulfilled love. And He wanted to give me what I missed. That was the love of Jesus.

Why am I not an atheist? Because of the book of God, the Bible that He used to speak to me. And I would like to explain to you why I am not an atheist by using a story from this book. It is a thrilling story about a boy who was sold as a slave but became a powerful ruler in Egypt, second only to Pharaoh. Even if you do not believe that this book is the Word of God, the story is interesting and beautiful. I invite you to look with me at that story so that I can further explain why I am not an atheist.

A STORY OF JEALOUSY

Joseph had many brothers. His father had two wives and that brought trouble. Joseph was the son of the favourite wife of his father. Therefore he was his favourite son. He gave only this son a beautiful robe, and there the problems started. His brothers became jealous.

True, that happens in every family when parents unwisely favour one of their children. But the jealousy of Joseph's ten brothers turned into hate. That was also Joseph's own fault. His behaviour was annoying. He sometimes gave his father a bad report about what his brothers did. He told them that he had dreamt that he would rule over them. And then it went terribly wrong. The Bible portrays it vividly:

> [Joseph's brothers] saw him in the distance, and before he reached them, they plotted to kill him. 'Here comes that dreamer!' they said to each other. 'Come now, let's kill him and throw him into one of these cisterns and say that a ferocious animal devoured him. Then we'll see what comes of his dreams.'

> When Reuben heard this, he tried to rescue him from their hands. 'Let's not take his life', he said. 'Don't shed any blood. Throw him into this cistern here in the wilderness, but don't lay a hand on him.' Reuben said this to rescue him from them and take him back to his father. So when Joseph came to his brothers, they stripped him of his robe – the ornate robe he was wearing – and they took him and threw him into the cistern. The cistern was empty; there was no water in it. As they sat down to eat their meal, they looked up and saw a caravan of Ishmaelites coming from Gilead. Their camels were loaded with spices, balm and myrrh, and they were on their way to take them down to Egypt.

> Judah said to his brothers, 'What will we gain if we kill our brother and cover up his blood? Come, let's sell him to the Ishmaelites and not lay our hands on him; after all, he is our brother, our own flesh and blood.' His brothers agreed. So when the Midianite merchants came by, his brothers pulled Joseph up out of the cistern and sold him for twenty shekels of silver to the Ishmaelites, who took him to Egypt. (Gen. 37:18-28)

The Bible tells about the people of God. It is not a story about heroes. Here we read about a father who is behaving not very wisely, a young Joseph who is spoiled by his father, and brothers who are jealous and hate him and want to kill their brother.

This is not the only story in the Bible that tells so openly the truth about people. On the first pages of the Bible, we already read about a man who wants to kill his brother. The Bible is very realistic. *Homo homini lupus est* is an old Latin phrase meaning 'man is a wolf to [his fellow] man'.

People can be very social and friendly. That is great. Sometimes it is impressive what people do for others. But in this world you also see the opposite. Jealousy and hatred rise up, and terrible things happen. You cannot trust people because there is something in us that can make us mean in no time. Be realistic. That is our world.

There are horrible examples in the history of the world. Names of countries like Rwanda or Yugoslavia remind us how neighbours became killers of one another.

Now I live as a Dutchman with my wife in Ukraine. I work here – just as my father did in Papua – as a missionary. I love the people and the country. People are friendly, the country is fascinating.

But the history here is terrifying. It is shocking to read and hear what people did to each other when totalitarian regimes came into these countries. Under Stalin and Hitler, millions of people were killed. Ukraine is one of the so-called 'bloodlands'.[1] Under Stalin, even before the Great War, millions died here in Ukraine of starvation.

Why was there a famine? Ukraine is a fertile country. Her black earth can produce a lot of grain. And it did. But the communists took all the food away from the people. They wanted to change society and oppressed the farmers. That famine, called 'Holodomor', was a terrible time in the 1930s in Ukraine. And then some years later the Germans came. Again millions of people were killed.

The reason I am not an atheist is because I do not trust man.

But don't misunderstand me. I am not asserting that I myself am better. When I say that I do not trust man, I include myself. I learned also not to trust myself. You can have some high standards or ideals and you can defend them or propagate them, but at the same time you may not be acting as you are talking. That is not good. You start to dislike yourself and you try to change. You try it, succeed sometimes, but also fail. And that becomes a real problem when

---

1   *Bloodlands*: *Europe Between Hitler and Stalin* is a book written by Timothy D. Snyder. The book is about the mass killing of an estimated 14 million non-combatants by the regimes of Joseph Stalin's Soviet Union and Adolf Hitler's Nazi Germany between the years 1933 and 1945 in a region which comprised what is modern-day Poland, Ukraine, Belarus, Russia and the Baltic states (Wikipedia).

you read the book of God, which is what I do. It is like a lamp that shows you the dark side of your character and behaviour. But it also tells us that there is Someone – much greater – who will help you.

Maybe you know the story of Johnny Cash and his struggle with amphetamines and barbiturates. He sang great songs about love, but experienced also the dark side of human nature in himself. In one of his songs, he explains his rejection of atheism by saying:

Yes, I came to believe in a power much higher than I.[2]

A STORY OF TEMPTATION
Let us return to the book that depicts for us the life of that young man named Joseph. His brothers sold him to merchants who took him to Egypt and sold him to an important official of the Pharaoh. He worked in the house of that official as an attendant because his master trusted him, and then the next thing happened:

Now Joseph was well-built and handsome, and after a while his master's wife took notice of Joseph and said, 'Come to bed with me!' But he refused. 'With me in charge', he told her, 'my master does not concern himself with anything in the house; everything he owns he has entrusted to my care. No one is greater in this house than I am. My master has withheld nothing from me except you, because you are his wife. How then could I do such a wicked thing and sin against God?'

And though she spoke to Joseph day after day, he refused to go to bed with her or even be with her. One day he went into the house to attend to his duties, and none of the household servants was inside. She caught him by his cloak and said, 'Come to bed with me!' But he left his cloak in her hand and ran out of the house.

When she saw that he had left his cloak in her hand and had run out of the house, she called her household servants. 'Look,' she said to them, 'this Hebrew has been brought to us to make sport of us! He came in here to sleep with me, but I screamed. When he heard me scream for help, he left his cloak beside me and ran out of the house.'

---

2   Johnny Cash wrote this song, *I came to believe.*

She kept his cloak beside her until his master came home. Then she told him this story: 'That Hebrew slave you brought us came to me to make sport of me. But as soon as I screamed for help, he left his cloak beside me and ran out of the house.' When his master heard the story his wife told him, saying, 'This is how your slave treated me,' he burned with anger. Joseph's master took him and put him in prison, the place where the king's prisoners were confined. (Gen. 39:6b-20)

This could make you an atheist: you do what you think God wants you to do and then you get into serious problems like Joseph, who was locked up in prison. He did not want to have sex with that married woman because he knew that it was a wicked thing against the will of God. The commandments of God are always good. But to keep them does not keep you from problems.

It is not because I want to avoid problems that I am a believer. That egotistic reason to believe will cause you problems, I promise you. I have known people who were atheists, people who came to a church because they were looking for a life without problems. When you want that, I think it will be better not to become a Christian. Christianity does not guarantee you a life without problems. No one lives without facing problems. Maybe you live in a part of the world where you do not realize how difficult life is for most people on earth, but when you live in Ukraine you see people struggling around you with many things. That is reality and it is sad.

Is that the only thing to say? No, there is also something else going on.

The best way I can illustrate that is by telling you what happened to Joseph. He really got into problems, but God was working in a special way. In prison, Joseph met officials of the Pharaoh, who were being punished by him. Joseph explained to them their dreams and his interpretations came true.

Later on, they brought Joseph to the Pharaoh, who also had a dream. Joseph interpreted the dream and explained that it was about an upcoming famine, and he gave Pharaoh good advice about how to prevent his people from dying from hunger. Pharaoh put Joseph in charge of the whole land of Egypt and many lives were saved. God was working all the time in Joseph's life in that direction.

That is the way God is dealing with the problems in this world. He does it in His way, not in our way. You know what the human way is to deal with the problems in this world – it is by power of force. When you have a bad situation as, for example, they thought it was in Iraq, then they change it by force. I was impressed by the power of the air forces. Saddam Hussein had no chance.

God can work in that way. He can show His power and He did. The Bible gives some examples. But He prefers to work with the power of love. He does not want to destroy, but He wants to save. And He did that in a mysterious way.

I am not an atheist because God works to save. His divine power was working when a man hung on the cross. He hung there as a criminal. Who could believe that God was doing a great work there? Who could ever accept that that beaten man up there was the Son of God? There was God. Let me be clear: it is strange for me too. I would also have scoffed there at the place where the cross stood; I would also have spat on the ground and walked away. But God opened my eyes to find Him – at the cross.

As Martin Luther states: 'A human being is not able to reach God with the help of wisdom or works, since God is hidden; the true wisdom and knowledge can be found only in the cross.'[3]

God's power was there – really, but hidden. There was suffering. There was a man dying among two others who also were crucified. But He was totally different, as His life had shown. He was the Son of God in power. He was the man of God in holiness. And He died there to bring forgiveness instead of punishment. That is the power of love that really changes life.

How? I am very impressed and touched by a story from South Africa. The time of apartheid was the time of the power of the whites against the blacks. What came after apartheid? Did we then

---

3   Quoted in *One With God: Salvation As Deification And Justification* by Veli-Matti Kärkkäinen, p. 43.

see the time of the power of the blacks against the whites? Was it the time of revenge? Of course, bad things happened, but there was also the power of love, the power of the cross.

Imagine this scene from a recent courtroom trial in South Africa: a frail black woman stands slowly to her feet. She is about 70 years of age. Facing her from across the room are several white police officers, one of whom, Mr van der Broek, has just been tried and found implicated in the murders of both the woman's son and her husband some years before.

And now the woman stands in the courtroom and listens to the confessions offered by Mr van der Broek. A member of South Africa's Truth and Reconciliation Commission turns to her and asks, 'So, what do you want? How should justice be done to this man who has so brutally destroyed your family?' 'I want three things,' begins the old woman, calmly but confidently. 'I want first to be taken to the place where my husband's body was burned so that I can gather up the dust and give his remains a decent burial.' She pauses, then continues. 'My husband and son were my only family. I want, secondly, therefore, for Mr van der Broek to become my son. I would like for him to come twice a month to the ghetto and spend a day with me so that I can pour out on him whatever love I still have remaining within me. And, finally,' she says, 'I want a third thing. I would like Mr van der Broek to know that I offer him my forgiveness because Jesus Christ died to forgive. This was also the wish of my husband. And so, I would kindly ask someone to come to my side and lead me across the courtroom so that I can take Mr van der Broek in my arms, embrace him and let him know that he is truly forgiven.'

As the court assistants come to lead the elderly woman across the room, Mr van der Broek, overwhelmed by what he has just heard, faints. And as he does, those in the courtroom, friends, family, neighbours – all victims of decades of oppression and injustice – begin to sing, softly, but assuredly, 'Amazing grace, how sweet the sound, that saved a wretch like me.'[4]

---

4   http://www.reformational.org.uk/index.php?option=com_content&task=view&id=92&
     Itemid=35.

That is the power of the love of God who heals and restores. That is what we need to find hope in a world full of destructive power.

A VISION OF HOPE

Joseph's brothers went to Egypt when there was famine in their own country. They were almost scared to death when they discovered that the mighty man on the throne was their brother Joseph. Now Joseph had the power to get revenge. But he had discovered in his life the power of God who was at work, and he said to his brothers:

> 'You intended to harm me, but God intended it for good to accomplish what is now being done, the saving of many lives. So then, don't be afraid. I will provide for you and your children'. And he reassured them and spoke kindly to them ... Then Joseph said to his brothers, 'I am about to die. But God will surely come to your aid and take you up out of this land to the land he promised on oath to Abraham, Isaac and Jacob'. And Joseph made the Israelites swear an oath and said, 'God will surely come to your aid, and then you must carry my bones up from this place'. So Joseph died at the age of a hundred and ten. And after they embalmed him, he was placed in a coffin in Egypt. (Gen. 50:20-21, 24-26)

Whoever discovers in his life that governing power of love finds a good reason to have hope. When God is working in your life to restore, He will finish it. He promised to give us a new life with a new body. Joseph believed that. Therefore, he wanted the Israelites to take his body to the promised land. There he was buried, waiting for the fulfilment of God's promise.

In the same way, I also want them to bury my body. Yes, I know that it will return to ashes. But God Almighty, who works with the power of love, will give me a new body, as He promises in His book. He will open a new world and then His children will receive the unfolding of the answer to their prayers and hopes and dreams.[5] We will see that nothing was in vain – not our problems, our joys, our tears, our labour.

---

5   Don Francisco sings about God's future in *Too Small A Price*.

I am not an atheist because I cannot and will not live without hope.

When my father was 63, he was diagnosed with stomach cancer. He was treated in the hospital and just at that time there was a camera team from a Dutch television network who interviewed people with cancer. And it struck them how some people found hope in their faith but others did not. So they interviewed my father, who told them about his hope. He knew that he would have the time of his life when the time of his life was over.

In that hope he died.

But the Dutch television network also interviewed a man who was an atheist. It was a kind of double-portrait. And in that broadcast you see him walking through his garden, and he points to an insect which flies one day and then disappears, and he says, 'That is our life – we live a short time as that insect does and then we die.' In that opinion he passed away.

Let me tell you. I cannot live with that. It would make me crazy. Nothing would have any sense: all my tears, my pain, my work, my joys – all in vain. Awful – without God, without hope.

I have lived now for some years in Ukraine. I see how many people live without hope. Many people are still atheists after the time of communism. In that time, they forced people to be atheists. One man told me how he came to believe and how his parents wanted to take him to a mental hospital. That time of communism is over. But many people still live without hope, some in poverty and some in luxury. In despair there is the vodka. Yes, alcohol makes you forget for a while. But next day in your headache you see still no hope, only a new bitter day with no sense. Is there real hope?

I think Jesus really gives hope. At the cross He died, but from the grave He rose after three days. In Him you can find life for ever.

That's why I am not an atheist – Jesus is stronger than death.

So I follow Him, in this life, but also through the grave to His future.

Join me!

4

A CEO
explains why she is not an Atheist

ELAINE DUNCAN

My job as the CEO of the Scottish Bible Society gives me the privilege of visiting other parts of the world and meeting people who live in circumstances, environments and cultures very different from my own. In this article I want to begin by telling the stories of some people I have met recently who have been an inspiration to me. Each has his/her own faith story and together they illustrate the international and trans-cultural mix of people who are persuaded that following Jesus is the best way to live life.

Let me introduce you to some of these people, before I relate them to my own experience – all in the endeavour to explain why I am not an atheist.

A CHINESE BELIEVER
John has lived all his life in China. He is in his early fifties. As a ten-year-old, he and his father found themselves in a secret meeting of Christians who were defying the communist government of the day. Under Chairman Mao, religion was to be eradicated from China. Churches were closed and if people had Bibles they had to hand them in so that they could be burned on bonfires in the centre of towns and villages. Many courageous Christians hid Bibles in

their homes, often behind bricks in the wall. They met secretly to study the Bible and to pray together.

It was to such a meeting that John and his dad were taken. John's mum had died when he was an infant and his life had been an incredibly tough experience. At this meeting, John learned of the Lord Jesus who loved him and who had died to rescue him. His ten-year-old understanding was stirred and he became a Christian. Today he runs a Christian bookshop in Nanjing. He regularly preaches in churches in his city. His life experience has been as different from mine as you could imagine, and I find myself challenged by his love and devotion to Jesus that has grown and matured over the years.

The Bible led John to Jesus and yet he is not able to sell the Bible in his bookshop. The distribution of the Bible in China is still controlled by the government and is only available through official churches. Religious freedom is allowed in China, but still not in the way we understand it in a Western democratic context. Yet the church is growing rapidly and many are turning to Christianity as their source of hope in the midst of challenging circumstances. To see and experience the sheer joy of people receiving their own Bible for the first time in a Chinese church is not an experience to be easily forgotten or dismissed.

China has moved on significantly since its Cultural Revolution (referred to today by the Chinese as 'the dark period of our history') but even so, there is no overt encouragement for people to become Christians. In some areas it is still very difficult and even dangerous for people to be followers of Jesus. So why do people fill the churches in droves? I believe it is because they encounter Jesus and find that He is the source of life and hope. Yes, of course there will be other factors at play – we are complex human beings. When Chinese Christians tell me why they are eager to have a Bible, it always involves some expression of wanting to know God better, of growing in their relationship with Him.

A KENYAN BELIEVER

Mary belongs to the Masai tribe and lives in a settled Masai community in the Rift Valley in Kenya. She is a young woman, married with six children. She is bright and intelligent, able in English as well as her own language. It is only in the last two years that she has learned to read and write. She had heard parts of the Bible read and found herself drawn to it more and more. She was frustrated because she could not access it for herself and had to rely on others to read it to her.

She talked with a local church pastor and found that he had been approached by the Bible Society in Kenya about starting literacy classes in the community. Mary's adventure of learning to read began, motivated by her hunger to know God better. She can now read the Bible for herself.

Mary's life has changed significantly since learning to read and write. She is now able to secure a wider range of jobs and therefore better provide for her family because of her newly learned skill.

Another consequence of being able to read for Mary is that she can check out what she hears taught in church. She does not want to be hoodwinked or deceived into believing things the Bible doesn't actually teach. She has a sharp mind and applies it to her growing relationship with God. I met her pastor, who verified that Mary keeps him on his toes as she interacts with his sermons!

Despite our very different life experiences, I find myself encouraged by Mary's thoughtful devotion to Jesus Christ. Her relationship with God has given her a fresh vision for her life and provided the motivation to stretch herself beyond what is 'normal' for women in her culture.

A Peruvian Believer

Boys often end up on the streets in Lima because men in Peru do not take their responsibilities as husbands and fathers very seriously. Often men leave the family home to seek a new life elsewhere. A mother can be left with six or eight mouths to feed and the challenge gets increasingly difficult. There comes a point when she has to face the agonizing decision of which of her children will cope best if put out of the home to fend for themselves. This happens frequently in the less affluent, rural areas. The ones put out of the home (usually boys) will then try to make their way to the capital city as they think they have a better chance of survival there. Scripture Union, a Christian charity, runs homes for such boys where they are cared for, sent to school and trained in a trade to help them on the road to independence.

One such teenager – let's call him Pedro – heard that one of the staff from the home was about to travel and would be visiting his home village. Pedro asked Peter if he would try to find his mum and deliver a letter he had written to her. He showed Peter the letter, and Peter then recounted it to me. In it, Pedro told his mum what had happened to him since he had left home (had been evicted!) and how he had been to school, was learning a trade and had a loving, caring environment to live in. He told her about his day-to-day life, his friends, some of his experiences. Then he wrote: 'I don't know if I'll ever see you again on earth, but I do know that if you become a friend of Jesus I'll see you in heaven.'

I found myself asking what power there is that can enable a teenage boy to write such a gracious and forgiving letter to his mum who put him out and left him to fend for himself at such an early age. Pedro had experienced the love of God in his life and it has changed his perspective on everything, including his own past and his relationships. He has discovered an inner strength that enables him to take the initiative and respond in a remarkably mature way towards his mother. I find his faith and trust in God compelling.

BRAZILIAN BELIEVERS

On a trip to Brazil I was taken to visit a prison. When we arrived at the large steel door at the entrance to the prison, we rang the bell. We heard the key turn in the lock and the door was opened to us by – a prisoner!

The prison is run as part of the official prison service in Brazil but with a very different philosophical approach compared to other prisons. This prison is run on the basis of biblical values and principles. Like most prisons, it has a high-security wing and more open areas. Prisoners are sent to this particular prison at the discretion of the judge hearing their case. Some of the older judges are sceptical; the younger ones tend to be the ones more open to try this very different approach.

The prisoners are taken through three stages of restorative justice, with the first step being to take ownership of the responsibility for their crime. This is done in the closed security area. It is a holistic approach in that the prisoner is treated as a full human being – with physical, emotional and spiritual dimensions. Support is given to the prisoners in each of these aspects of life. There is an emphasis at this stage too on rebuilding family and social contacts.

The second stage is in a semi-open environment where inmates are given training and work opportunities within the prison. I saw a bakery, a farm and a shoemaking operation in full swing.

The final stage, for those who have responded well to being given responsibility and have shown they can be trusted, provides opportunities for work outside the prison with a return to the cells (dormitories) in the evening.

Very few of the members of staff working in the prison are paid. They are involved in the administrative running of the establishment. Everything else is run by the prisoners themselves. Compared with other prisons, this one is much cheaper to run and also has greatly reduced reoffending rates. The whole atmosphere was marked by respect for oneself and others. Obviously not everyone becomes a Christian while an inmate, but many do and find that they experience a new freedom in life, even before they are released.

Seeing the impact of Christian/biblical values lived out in the context of a prison was inspiring. It is my conviction that Christianity is not just good for individuals, but for families and for communities too. What an encouragement to see this in action in the tough environment of a prison.

My Own Story

These are four people whose stories I have found inspirational and encouraging.

But why is it that I find their stories so compelling?

Some people may think I am simply having my own world view reinforced and so I am bound to be encouraged. That is true.

However, I think there is something deeper going on too. I like to consider myself a 'thinking' Christian and endeavour not to take what might be called a 'blind faith' approach to what I believe (though there are areas of mystery that I accept on trust). So, in my encounters with people in other cultures, I am trying to listen and understand what has led them to where they are now. In each and every case, the reality and impact of their relationship with Jesus Christ is the common thread. He is the reason for their faith and belief. He is their source of love and forgiveness. He is their hope. He brings them into the light and truth.

I am now in my fifties and became a convinced Christian as a young teenager. I did not have much trouble believing what I had been taught in Sunday School as it was communicated enthusiastically and with conviction.

A turning point for me in my early teens was the realization that the facts I believed about God from the Bible led to a relationship with God. Something 'clicked' in my young mind – a realization that Christianity is not simply a philosophy of life or a good moral framework to live by. It is all about a relationship with the living God. So from that point, what I believed took on deeper and wider dimensions because it was being worked out in and through a relationship with God, and relationships are dynamic, constantly changing.

THE QUESTION OF TRUTH

Back in the 1970s and 1980s as I went through school, college and then worked with students in higher education, a key question about anything was, Is it true? – can whatever is being purported be verified? We were truly children of the Enlightenment!

So, the question of the historical reality of Jesus and the validity of the gospel accounts of His life, death and resurrection was very important to me.

I remember getting very excited about Frank Morison's book *Who Moved the Stone?* As a bright, intelligent lawyer, he realized that Christianity could be discredited if the resurrection of Jesus could be disproved and he set out to do just that.

His book gives the account of how his diligent research led him to conclude that the historical evidence for the resurrection weighs heavier on the 'it happened' side of the scale than the 'it didn't happen' side of the scale. The consequence for him personally was to become a Christian.

I used to spend many happy hours debating the truth of the resurrection in student union bars with eager searching minds. The conversations would range around many different topics but usually ended with the question, 'So what do you do with Jesus, His life, death and resurrection?' – posed to those who were enthusiastic atheists.

The Testing of Faith

As I have developed through my thirties and forties different questions have become more (or as) important to me and to those around me. For example, does Christianity actually work? Can it be authenticated in my own life and in the lives of other followers of Jesus? I guess this boils down to asking, 'Is it real?'

This was tested personally for me in painful experiences such as:

- the death of my mum,

- the breakdown of significant relationships and then the restoration of (most!) of those relationships,

- disappointment and grief as I witnessed others fail and fall,

- the struggle with inner temptations that led to me failing and falling,

- challenges in the workplace that caused serious stress and tension.

These were times when it felt as if my faith and trust in a living God were on the line. Could I really believe and trust what I was reading in the Bible? Did God really care about me? Was His Holy Spirit really living within me, making Jesus real and giving me strength to hold on in the midst of mental turmoil and emotional despair?

The journey in all these situations was a tough one. In many of them I railed against God, hurling big questions at Him while not really being open to getting any answers and certainly not any I liked!

THE REALISM OF THE BIBLE

During this period of my life my appreciation of the richness and depth of the Bible grew enormously. Out of the rawness of some of my own experiences I found resonance with characters in both the Old and New Testaments. I realized that the way God speaks to us through the Bible is real and authentic. What I mean is that the human characters, through whom God's story is told, are not presented as perfect, but as flawed human beings just like me. They too were portrayed as having to grapple with that vexed thing called 'human nature' and had to work out their relationship with God (or lack of relationship with Him) in a host of challenging situations.

Reading the Bible helped me to repeatedly hear God's invitation to come to Him with my mess, my misery and my musings, and to be assured that I wouldn't be turned away. It also helped me realize that my issues and challenges would not disappear overnight, but rather they would be used to shape me and deepen my relationship with Jesus.

THE EFFECTS OF FAITH

In the last few years, partly because of some of the work we do in taking the Bible into the public square, I have found myself more and more convinced of how good the impact of the Bible and Christianity can be.

Over the centuries there have been glorious examples of this, and currently one of our educational resources helps schoolchildren to consider the impact of the Bible on Scottish culture and history. As Christians have taken the Bible seriously it has shaped our justice system, it has inspired our education system, it has shaped our approach to health and motivated care for those trapped in poverty, the marginalized and the otherwise neglected. This has shaped Scotland. Scottish Christians have also taken these values around the world.

It is also true that over the centuries there have been inglorious examples of how Christian belief and the Bible can be misused in abusive ways. These atrocities cannot be justified by anything I read and understand in the Bible. I struggle to make sense of some of these ambiguities. However, it would not be fair for the bad examples to negate the good examples, which are, I think, in the overwhelming majority.

I watched a DVD recently where the question was posed: what would the world have been like if the church had not existed for the last 2000 years? It's a difficult, hypothetical question to answer! For sure, followers of Jesus regularly get things wrong – but they also regularly get things right. The main subject of the DVD is an exploration of the enormous impact that Jesus Christ has had on the world. My heart warms as I consider that,

• no other figure in history has brought about such changes in the way people think and behave;

• no other person has been responsible for the transformation of so many lives;

• no other person loves me as fully and as completely as He does;

• no other person has died in my place so that I can joyfully spend eternity with Him;

• no other person is so ready to forgive me and not write me off because I am slow, stupid, selfish and stubborn;

• no other person gives me the kind of vision for my life that He gives;

• no one else brings the hope He brings;

• no one else helps me sing in the dark like He does;

• no one else is my constant companion.

People who know and love Jesus Christ really do make an impact in the world and it is an impact for good. The values that Jesus lived transform communities and cultures, and can be lived out and find expression in all cultures around the world.

I am not an atheist because I know and love Jesus Christ. I am convinced He is alive and well, and through all that He has done He enables me to belong in relationship with God – Father, Son and Holy Spirit. I have found my home, my identity, my reason for being.

The message of the Bible makes sense to me, even though I do not understand it all. I find it to be true, to be real and to be good. I am glad I belong to the community of God's people around the world. I certainly have no regrets about believing in God and thus experiencing such a strong outpouring of love, grace, mercy and happiness.

5

A PASTOR
explains why he is not an Atheist

ALEX MACDONALD

An advertizing campaign run by Richard Dawkins and others in 2009 said: 'There's probably no God. Now stop worrying and enjoy your life.'

But is God's probable non-existence a cause for not worrying? A leading intellectual atheist of the twentieth century, Bertrand Russell, said he had to read a detective story a day to divert him from the fear that mankind was going to destroy the world.

And anyway, is the belief that human life and the universe are going to be extinguished in darkness for ever a cause for not worrying?

I would like to tell you why I am not an atheist. And I hope what I have to say may be helpful to you if you are wondering why you should believe in God.

The cynic might say right away, 'I can tell you why you are not an atheist – it's because you are a preacher and you have a professional interest in keeping God alive'! But, of course, I was not always a preacher; I was not always a Christian. So I would like to explain why I believe that God does exist and what difference it makes in my life and the lives of many others.

73

WHY I MIGHT HAVE BEEN AN ATHEIST

Like many people of my generation, I have felt the lure of atheism at various points and in its many forms: from pantheism – the belief that the universe is God, that there is not a personal God at all – to ideologies like Marxism and communism, stressing social justice and what man can achieve. So I would like to consider first the reasons why I might have been an atheist.

Take freedom, for instance. I was brought up in a Highland Free Church home. For some people that has been something to put them off Christianity, to put them off religion, to put them off believing in God. They have had some kind of Christian or church background and their reaction to it has been negative, leading them to believe there is no God.

But in fact I spent my teenage years, which are probably the most rebellious period of anyone's life, away from home. That is because in the part of the Highlands I came from to go to ordinary secondary school you had to leave home, live in lodgings in a town many miles away and attend school there. So, what I did rebel against at that particular point in my life was not what I would regard now as true Christianity but what would be called bourgeois values: the idea of a kind of respectable, middle-class view of what religion and morality is, which now I would see as a Christless religion and a loveless morality. It was not at all what I have come to know as the truth that God reveals in the Bible.

This was the sixties, a time of longing for freedom, breaking free from all kind of restrictions. So many of the songs of that period expressed that longing, but some honestly expressed pessimism of ever finding true freedom, like Leonard Cohen's *Bird on the Wire*. There was the idea that there was no longer any meaning to life. The world seemed so horrendous in many ways, especially with the threat of the hydrogen bomb and nuclear warfare. What meaning could life have? Science itself seemed to have developed into some kind of great, destructive juggernaut. It had disappointed our expectations and failed to provide the answers that we were looking for. And because life, it was thought, had no meaning, there was also no point in morality, no point in believing in what is right or wrong.

It could all be summed up in the words of the nineteenth-century Russian novelist Dostoyevsky: 'Without God … everything is allowed.'[1] That was generally the idea in the sixties; it was called the permissive society. But the atheist writer Aldous Huxley once said:

> I had motives for not wanting the world to have a meaning; consequently assumed that it had none … For me, as, no doubt, for most of my contemporaries, the philosophy of meaninglessness was essentially an instrument of liberation. The liberation we desired was simultaneously liberation from a certain political and economic system and liberation from a certain system of morality.[2]

In other words, he wanted to break free and so he believed life had no meaning. It was not that he came intellectually to the honest belief that life had no meaning and, therefore, he could live any way he liked. He wanted to live any way he liked and, therefore, he said life had no meaning. So there was a certain amount of dishonesty going on at that time – and there still is.

But if we look carefully at that famous statement of Dostoyevsky's, 'If God does not exist, everything is permitted', and look at it the way he intended, we realize that, in fact, everything is not permitted. If I look at my life and say, 'Well, I would like to be as free as possible and I'd like to do everything I want to do', I cannot logically grant the same freedom to everyone else, because if everyone else does what they want to do they will impinge on my freedom. And I do not like other people doing the same things that I let myself off with.

There is some kind of standard that we come up against, irrespective of what we really might like. There are certain standards of right and wrong; everything is not permitted. The most liberated

---

1   Fyodor Dostoyevsky, *The Brothers Karamazov* (Penguin, 1982), Part 4, Book 11, Chapter 4, p. 691, (usually quoted as: 'If there is no God, everything is permitted').

2   Aldous Huxley, *Ends and Means* (London: Chatto & Windus, 1946), pp. 270 and 273.

person – the person who believes that the world is meaningless – if you treat her unfairly, she will complain and say, 'That's wrong! That's not fair.'

That is the kind of unwritten law that is there: there is some kind of idea of fairness, of right and wrong. Everything is not permitted. So, if everything is not permitted, is the logical conclusion, yes, God does exist, and there is some source of standards in this world?

THE PROBLEM OF SUFFERING

But a second reason why I might have been an atheist lies in the area of suffering and injustice. Like many others I was aware of the cruelty of the world, even from an early age – in nature, red in tooth and claw, or in human beings' treatment of one another. These are things of which we become conscious very early on, and as we get older there are various things that reinforce our awareness.

Again in the part of the world I come from, in the north of Scotland, there was a consciousness of past history, an injustice done in the past at the time of what is called the Highland Clearances, when many of the people were turned out of their homes and great sheep farms were set up instead. These people had to eke out a living on the coasts or they were transported away to America and Canada. Many of them died on the voyage; others arrived at the other side and eventually settled down there and made good lives. But there was this sense of injustice, of something wrong with a world where this kind of thing could happen.

Now that, of course, is magnified many times over throughout the whole world and there are examples in human history – in recent human history – far more horrific than the Clearances. The most notorious of all is the Holocaust: the attempted destruction of the Jewish people and others by the Nazis in Germany and the surrounding areas in Europe in the time leading up to and during the Second World War. The case against God, it has been said, can be summed up in two words – 'the Holocaust'. Such great suffering and injustice demonstrates that there is no God. There is such injustice in the world, there is such suffering – how could there be a good, all-powerful Being looking after everything?

76

Richard Dawkins says in *River out of Eden*: 'In a universe of blind physical forces and genetic replication, some people are going to get hurt, other people are going to get lucky, and you won't find any rhyme or reason to it, nor any justice. The universe we observe has precisely the properties we should expect if there is, at bottom, no design, no purpose, no evil, no good, nothing but blind pitiless indifference.'[3]

What effect will these ideas have? On respectable middle-class academics, probably very little. But what about an atheist experiment on whole societies?

But wait a minute! We had such an experiment in the twentieth century. Communism, which rejected Christian truth and values, conducted such an experiment, with disastrous consequences.

Ultimately there is no easy answer to the question of suffering, and I do not pretend to have one. But we have to ask: who caused the Holocaust? The Holocaust was caused by Nazis holding a particular philosophy and outlook on life that was essentially atheistic. They did not believe in God. They believed in human power. They may have sometimes used religious language, but they were avowedly anti-Christian.

If we look at the twentieth century – the countless millions of people who were killed – it was achieved by various branches of atheistic thought, not just Nazism on the Right, but also various forms of communism on the Left. In communist Russia and Eastern Europe, sixty million people were killed in fifty years, in China seventy million, and this was repeated in various other places to a lesser extent. So when we talk about what has caused such evil, we see not only that it is human beings, but particularly in the last century we have seen this unprecedented destruction and savagery unleashed by atheistic philosophies.

We also have to consider this: if there is no God, as Dostoyevsky said, everything is permitted. If there is no God, if there is no ultimate being to whom we are answerable, then how can we complain about anything? We cannot say that the Holocaust was

---

3   Richard Dawkins, *River out of Eden* (Basic Books, 1995), p. 132.

wrong, we cannot complain, we cannot plead for justice anywhere, we just have to accept that life is utterly meaningless.

Yet we do not. We cry out against the injustice of it. That seems to speak again of the fact that we have intrinsically a sense of justice, the sense that there is something unfair, the sense that some wrong has been done, and the more we complain about it and say, 'How could God exist and allow this?', the more we are actually complaining to God, because we believe in an ultimate standard of justice.

I also found the theoretical underpinnings of atheism unconvincing, particularly the belief in naturalism – the belief that everything can be explained by natural cause and effect, and there is no need for the supernatural.

But the eminent evolutionary biologist, J. B. S. Haldane, long ago pointed out the problem posed by naturalism for human rationality: 'If my mental processes are determined wholly by the motions of atoms in my brain, I have no reason to suppose that my beliefs are true ... and hence I have no reason for supposing my brain to be composed of atoms.'[4]

Interestingly, Charles Darwin applied similar doubt to his belief in God: could he trust a brain evolved from lower animals? But of course, the argument would apply to all his ideas, including evolution and natural selection!

Naturalism is self-contradictory. At least one thing does exist apart from the physical – the human ability to reason. The question we all have to answer is: where does our ability to reason come from?

THE LURE OF PANTHEISM

Another avenue along which I was tempted very strongly towards a form of atheism was pantheism. Pantheism means there is no personal God, but the universe is in some sense divine. There is a mystery about the universe itself and when we see its beauty we realize we are involved in some way in this great process.

---

4   J. B. S. Haldane, *Possible Worlds* (Transaction Publishers, 1927), p. 209.

I came at that view from perhaps a different angle from most people. During the sixties many people were drawn to Eastern religion and, although I did study Eastern philosophy at university, it was particularly through the writings of Neil Gunn, the Scottish novelist, that I came in contact with a certain form of pantheism, a Celtic mysticism which gave the impression that the universe is somehow spiritual.

When you read Neil Gunn, there is always this kind of mystery element in the natural world and in human beings' relation with it. It is something that is very appealing and very tempting: the idea that there is ultimately no personal God to whom you are answerable, but there is a kind of spirituality, a sense of awe – that feeling of the hairs at the back of your neck standing on end and of something exciting in this world, though it is vague and you cannot pin it down.

But if this is true, or if some form of pantheism is true – if the universe is divine and we are part of it – then ultimately there is no reason for a distinction between good and evil. If everything is part of God, whatever God is, we are simply saying we are all part of this universe and everything that happens is part of it, whether it is good or evil.

So how are we to decide what is good or evil? In Hinduism, which is more consistently pantheistic than any other form of thought, the emphasis is that all distinctions are illusory, so the distinction between good and evil is also an illusion. Everything ultimately is part of the One. And so we lose this firm line between good and evil which is so essential, not just to our other complaints about the existence of God, but to our whole lives. How can we live without some sense of good and evil, of right and wrong, without the ability to condemn, even if it is condemning others while letting ourselves off? We have this sense that there is this essential distinction between good and evil.

THE QUESTION OF SCIENCE

Another area where I might very well have become atheistic was the area of science – and this is true for very many people. The idea, put in the most popular terms, is that science has replaced God. Science and God are antagonistic to each other. Either science has disproved God in some way, or belief in God is anti-science.

But this ignores the origin of modern science. Joseph Needham looked at why modern science began in Western Europe and not in China. In many ways China had the technological ability. He says: 'There was no confidence that the code of Nature's laws could ever be unveiled and read, because there was no assurance that a divine being, even more rational than ourselves, had ever formulated such a code capable of being read.'[5]

Philosophers of science, such as Alfred North Whitehead and Robert Oppenheimer, stressed that science was born out of a Christian world view. This is a generally held view by historians of science. C. S. Lewis put it in a nutshell: 'Men became scientific because they expected Law in Nature, and they expected Law in Nature because they believed in a Legislator.'[6]

Early scientists saw their science as entirely consistent with their belief in God. Galileo actually defended the compatibility of Copernicus and the Bible: 'Holy Scripture and nature equally proceed from the divine Word, the first as dictated by the Holy Spirit, the second as the very faithful executor of God's commands.'[7]

In addition, leading scientists have been, and continue to be, Christians. Of the three greatest names in physics – Isaac Newton, James Clerk Maxwell and Albert Einstein – Newton and Clerk Maxwell were both committed Christians.

The complementary relationship between science and faith is well illustrated by the story told on page 25: a scientist and a boy scout, while walking along a cliff top, see a red flare out at sea. The scientist calculates the intensity, wavelength and luminosity of the light, while the boy scout recognizes it as an SOS signal and calls

---

5   Joseph Needham, *The Grand Titration* (Toronto: University of Toronto Press, 1969), p. 327.

6   C. S. Lewis, *Miracles: a preliminary study* (London: Collins, 1947), p. 110.

7   Galileo Galilei, *Letter to Father Benedetto Castelli*, 21 December 1613 (as quoted in http://www.vatican.va/holy_father/john_paul_ii/encyclicals/documents/hf_jp-ii_enc_15101998_fides-et-ratio_en.html, accessed 26.02.2013).

the coastguard! Both approaches discovered truth. One was entirely physical while the other dealt in meaning.

Science is limited to the physical. There is a great danger of reductionism – what Professor Donald MacKay called 'nothin-buttery', as if the scientist were to say that the flashing light was 'nothing but' light waves. Science and theology are complementary, not contradictory.

However, for many, evolution has replaced God. Richard Dawkins holds that natural selection is the blind watchmaker.

But nothing is straightforward in this area. Evolutionary biologist D. M. S. Watson said: 'The theory of evolution is a theory universally accepted, not because it can be proved by logically coherent evidence to be true, but because the only alternative is special creation, which is clearly incredible.'[8] What people may present as truth is not necessarily based on strong evidence, but is a result of their presuppositions (their faith).

The late Colin Patterson, who was a senior palaeontologist at the British Museum of Natural History, commented in a letter to Luther Sunderland on the lack of direct illustration of evolutionary transitions (missing links) in a book he had written (*Evolution*, 1978):

> If I knew of any, fossil or living, I would certainly have included them ... I will lay it on the line – there is not one such fossil for which one could make a watertight argument ... It is easy enough to make up stories of how one form gave rise to another, and to find reasons why the stages should be favoured by natural selection. But such stories are not part of science, for there is no way to put them to the test.[9]

Although at the popular level evolution is seen as explaining away any need for God, there are many scientists who entertain serious doubts on various areas of evolutionary theory. This inevitably

---

8   D. M. S. Watson, *Nature*, vol.127, p. 233.

9   Quoted in Luther Sunderland, *Darwin's Enigma* (Arkansas: Master Books, 1998), pp. 101-102 (Patterson's letter was written in 1979). Although much controversy surrounds quotations from Patterson, there is little doubt that he expressed scepticism about evolution.

WHY I AM NOT AN ATHEIST

militates against building an evolutionary philosophy offering a complete explanation of how the world has developed.

Richard Dawkins holds that natural selection ('the survival of the fittest') explains the development of life on earth, and that therefore it is 'a self-bootstrapping crane which eventually raised the world ... into its present complex existence', and that it is 'consciousness-raising' as to how the universe began and to explain human life.[10]

I readily grant that it is possible that natural selection can explain some aspects of the development of life. My father was a shepherd and his breeding of sheep was based on the fact that large variations can take place in a genetic pool. But it is a huge leap of faith to believe that this explains the origin of life and indeed the origin of the universe. Nor can natural selection and 'selfish genes' explain many aspects of human life such as altruism and self-sacrifice.

But the central objection to the existence of God in Dawkins's *The God Delusion* is, 'Who designed the designer?' This is the child's question, 'Who made God?' There is a mistake in the question. A created God is not the God of the Bible – He is uncreated, eternal. Dawkins's argument is an argument against a straw man.

Dawkins's answer to this is that it is a cop-out to say that by definition God is uncreated. He says that God's existence is more improbable than the improbability of the origin of life on earth or the improbability of the Big Bang resulting in the complex universe we observe today. He quotes the oft-used illustration of a hurricane in a scrapyard producing a Boeing 747. That is extremely improbable by pure chance.

This is a version of David Hume's argument that if something has only happened once, it is infinitely improbable. However, just because something is improbable, that doesn't mean it isn't true or doesn't exist. The universe may be highly or even infinitely improbable, but it does exist!

---

10   Richard Dawkins, *The God Delusion* (London: Transworld Publishers, 2007), p. 185.

MORE POSITIVELY ...

So, as I examined the various temptations to atheism I experienced, I found none of them satisfying. But my reasons for not being an atheist are not only negative. I believe there is positive evidence that God exists.

I BELIEVE IN GOD BECAUSE OF THE UNIVERSE

The existentialist philosopher Martin Heidegger argued that the basic philosophical question is, 'Why is there something instead of nothing?'[11] That may seem very obvious, but, in fact, it is the starting point. Something exists. The universe is here. We have not created it. We are here. We are part of the universe and we must make some sort of sense of it.

But what is there is not just something, it is this incredibly ordered and beautiful and human universe. It is ordered, in the sense that we can discover uniformity in it and frame scientific laws about it. It is beautiful, in that we can appreciate the beauty of the natural world and of human beings.

But it is also a kind of human universe, and even in science there is the development of what is called the anthropic principle, the idea that things seem to be fitting together in relation to human beings. And this is what we discover: that the world is there for our benefit and that there are all sorts of things that fit together for us. We discover and invent all sorts of things from the universe. We develop our life and our culture from it. It all seems to fit together. Now this poses a huge question: why should it be so? The universe does not seem to be random and utterly meaningless.

The physicist Roger Penrose (who worked with Stephen Hawking, the author of *A Brief History of Time*) computed the odds of the 'Big Bang' producing our ordered universe merely by accident. The odds came out at one in $10^{10(123)}$.[12] I am not a great mathematician but I know that that is a very big number! In fact,

---

11 M. Heidegger, *An Introduction to Metaphysics* (New Haven and London: Yale University Press, 1959), pp. 7-8.

12 Roger Penrose, *The Emperor's New Mind* (Oxford University Press, 1989), pp. 339-45.

we are assured that it is so large that it has more zeros than the total number of particles in the entire universe.

In other words, he is saying that it is impossible that the universe as it is could have come about by accident. There seems to be some sort of design at work in the physical universe from the moment of the 'Big Bang' or however we describe its beginning. And it is interesting that science at the moment is definitely pointing towards the universe having had a beginning, and a structured beginning, although we cannot fully understand it – which is exactly what the Bible says.

Voltaire, the French philosopher, said: 'I shall always be convinced that a watch proves a watchmaker and a universe proves a God.'[13] That argument is often ridiculed and people say that, if it is valid, all it shows is that a universe proves a universe-maker, which is different from a God. But if there is a Being – whatever we call Him, Universe-maker or anything else – who has made this universe, this amazing, vast, complex, beautiful universe, then I will fall down and worship Him. Voltaire and others have seen the power of this argument from design. The universe seems to be designed. It is not just chaotic, not just random, not just by accident. There seems to be some meaning and purpose behind it.

In the very first words of the Bible we have the explanation of this: 'In the beginning God created the heavens and the earth.' The first verse of Genesis does not explain the mechanisms by which God did it. It may be the 'Big Bang'; it may be that modern physicists are on the right lines in explaining how God brought the universe into being. But we are simply told the fact that it did not have an impersonal, chance beginning. God decided it and God designed it and God created it, by whatever mechanism. Similarly with the history of the universe – God has designed it, God has created it, God is working out His purposes in it. And this to my mind makes sense of what we see in the universe. I am not an atheist because of the universe.

---

13   Quoted by H. N. Brailsford, *Voltaire* (Oxford University Press, 1935), p. 122.

I BELIEVE IN GOD BECAUSE OF HUMAN BEINGS

I am not an atheist because of the nobility of human beings. We have thought already about the cruelty and the evil of the human world, but what about the nobility? 'How like a god!' Hamlet says[14] – of a human being, of a man – how like a god. And there is much in human history that brings out the same emphasis. There is the creativity of human beings. If we look at Michelangelo's statue of David or any of the great works of art, the gift of creativity that human beings have is breathtaking. If we look at York Minster, we see a medieval building that is astonishing today as we take in its complexity and soaring beauty. Or as we look at modern inventions like satellites or television or computers or whatever, we are amazed at the creativity of human beings.

But there is also a moral awareness that I have emphasized already. We have this awareness of right or wrong. We have what is called a conscience. Yes, there may be great evil and great brutality in the world, but there is always a voice raised against it. There is something within us that says this is wrong, this is evil. There is something about us as human beings which seems inexplicable in purely mechanistic or animal terms.

Supremely, there is love. I do not mean the kind of love of which we might see parallels in the animal world, such as my cat loving me because I feed it cat food. There is something much superior in the human world where love may be shown without anything gained in return – for example in times of war, when people sacrificed their own lives for other people's freedom. But examples occur also in times of peace – a mother dying for her children, people giving their lives or living their lives for other people, sacrificially, unselfishly. What is the explanation of it, how is there such nobility in human beings?

In contrast with that, we thought earlier about the cruelty and brutality that exists in the human condition. The psychologist, B. F. Skinner, satirized Shakespeare when he said of man: 'How like

---

14   William Shakespeare, *Hamlet*, Act 2, Scene 2 (http://shakespeare.mit.edu/hamlet/full.html, accessed 26.02.2013).

a dog!'[15] He was comparing human beings to animals and showing how animal psychology can teach us a great deal about human beings. But human beings are capable of far greater brutality or cruelty than any animal. A human being is capable of far more evil than a dog. As Dostoyevsky said, it is unfair to talk of bestial cruelty – a tiger would never dream of nailing a man by his ears.[16] There is something intrinsically and worryingly evil in the heart of human beings, so that even the most respectable person might commit some incredible wickedness. There is all the spite and the hurt and the abuse in this world just at the ordinary level of human society, let alone the great, horrific things like the Holocaust, or Bosnia, or Kosovo, or Rwanda.

What is the explanation of this paradox – that there is this great nobility of human beings, these great achievements of human beings, and yet this cruelty and evil? I have never found a satisfactory explanation in any kind of atheistic thinking.

The satisfying explanation I have discovered is the message that the Bible gives me – that we as human beings are made in the image of God. We are personal beings, not just some kind of advanced animal, not just some kind of computer. We are human beings made in the image of God – personal, spiritual beings with capacities of creativity and of love and moral awareness. We are Godlike. How like a God – Shakespeare was right.

But, on the other hand, the Bible also explains why there is evil. God did not originally create us evil. He created us perfectly good, to enjoy the universe that He had made and to enjoy fellowship with Him. But we rebelled against Him. The origin of evil is rebellion. The origin of all the evil in the world is rebellion against the laws and the love of God – the refusal to put God in God's place, at the centre, and the resolve to place ourselves at the centre. And then we make the absolute mess that we have made of the world and of our

---

15   B. F. Skinner, *Beyond Freedom and Dignity* (Indianapolis: Hackett Publishing Company, 1971), p. 201.

16   Fyodor Dostoyevsky, *The Brothers Karamazov* (New York: The Modern Library, n.d.), p. 293.

lives. To my mind, this explanation we discover in the Bible is the most satisfying explanation as to who we are: made in the image of God, but sinners, rebels against Him.

I Believe in God Because of the Bible

I have referred already to some of the things it says. It is because of this book that I am not an atheist. This is an amazing book. It is remarkable because of its survival. What other book of the ancient world – and we are talking here of 2,000 to 3,500 years ago – has survived in the way the Bible has? We have bits and pieces of manuscripts and books of the ancient world, but they are in libraries or museums, and they are of no great interest to most ordinary people.

This book is of astonishing interest to people, and it has survived down through the ages. In spite of vitriolic attacks against it, in spite of attempts to suppress it, it has survived and it flourishes. It is still the world's best seller. Back in the sixties, people were glibly saying that the Bible was being outsold by another book – 'the little red book', *The Thoughts of Chairman Mao*. It might have been very popular for a short time, but it has disappeared. Nobody thinks about it now, nobody talks about it, hardly anyone reads it, but the Bible has increased its popularity. Even in China, where attempts were made to root out the Bible, it is going from strength to strength.

This book is also amazing because of its unity and complexity. The Bible is a complex book. I am not going to pretend that you can simply just pick it up and start reading it anywhere and you will understand everything right away. It contains 66 books, written by about forty authors, so it is complicated. It was written over a period of at least 1,500 years by all these different people living in different cultures, writing in three different languages, and yet – this is the amazing thing – it all fits together. You can read it as one story. It has one purpose. It has one focus – Jesus Christ. No one human being or group of human beings could have engineered that. It came together over a period of a millennium and a half, from Moses right through to the apostle John. And yet it makes sense. It has a power today that no other book has.

Of course there are those who describe the Bible, even the Gospels, as myth, and so deduce it is not to be taken seriously. C. S. Lewis (whose academic expertise was in literature) demolished this position in his *Fern-seed and Elephants* (1959) in reference to John's Gospel: 'I have been reading poems, romances, vision literature, legends, myths, all my life. I know what they are like. I know that not one of them is like this.'[17] He says there are only two possibilities: the author is either reporting what happened, or else someone nearly 2000 years ago suddenly invented modern, novelistic, realistic narrative! He obviously discounts the latter possibility.

The Bible's reliability has also been shown by the discoveries of archaeology. A great archaeologist from the beginning of the twentieth century, Sir William Ramsay, started off his investigations in the Middle East and in Turkey convinced that the Bible was inaccurate and unreliable. That was because of the kind of teaching about it that he had had at university. But when he investigated for himself, when he actually excavated in those ancient cities and pieced it all together, he confirmed the details of Luke's record in the Acts of the Apostles time and time again. His conclusion was that Luke should be placed along with the very greatest of historians. He came to view what Luke said as completely accurate.

Probably the most famous vindication of the accuracy of the New Testament concerns Gallio whom Luke says was proconsul of Achaia (Acts 18:12). Gallio was the well-known brother of Seneca, and classical scholars doubted the accuracy of Luke's account because there was no other record of his being proconsul of Achaia. However, archaeologists discovered an inscription at Delphi in Greece, which not only proved that he was indeed proconsul, but even gives the date which can be pinpointed to A.D. 51–52! Instead of being an embarrassing example of the unreliability of the Bible, this verse has become a kingpin in dating the events of the New Testament.

---

17   C. S. Lewis, *Fern-seed and Elephants: and other essays on Christianity* (Glasgow: Collins, Fount Paperbacks, 1977), p. 108.

So we have this remarkable book that has survived, that has this internal unity, this reliability and this amazing popularity throughout the world. It is a book that commands our attention. And because of this book and its message, I believe that God exists: that this is God speaking to me. It has a vibrant, abiding and powerful message for every one of us.

I BELIEVE IN GOD BECAUSE OF JESUS

There is a passage in 1 John, chapter 4, which speaks about Jesus, and about the love of God. 'God is love, and this is the love that he has shown to us, that he sent his one and only Son into the world so that we might live through him. This is love, not that we loved God, but that he loved us and sent his Son as an atoning sacrifice for our sins.' I am not an atheist, because of Jesus. I am not an atheist, because I have come to know God's love to me in Jesus Christ.

I have come to know that love in different ways. First of all, I came to know it through my family. One of the strongest reasons why I am not an atheist is that this love of God in Jesus Christ was communicated to me from a very early age, and I became aware of the great message of the love of God in Jesus Christ – that 'God so loved the world that He gave His only begotten Son so that whoever believes in Him should not perish but have eternal life' (John 3:16, NKJV). I have come to know that love through my wife and family, through Christian friends, through the support and encouragement of Christian people, in ways that have been astonishing and beyond the call of duty, love that has not been shown by anyone else.

But supremely I have become aware of this love of God directly in Jesus Christ. The message of the Bible focuses on Jesus, this unique person who is the Son of God. He made extraordinary claims about Himself, such as, 'I and the Father are one' (John 10:30). He said all sorts of outrageous things.

And remember He was saying these things, not in India in the context of Hinduism where people would say, 'Oh yes, we are all one with God', but amongst the most monotheistic people in the whole history of the world, the Jewish people – and He Himself was a Jew. There is one God, only one God – one God, who is high, majestic and holy, above this world and above human beings – yet he said: 'I and the Father are one' (John 10:30). When at his trial He was put on oath and asked: 'Are you the Son of the Blessed, are you the Son of God?', He said, 'I am' (Mark 14:61f). Nothing could be clearer than that Jesus presented Himself as the Son of God – the revelation of God in this world, God become flesh.

Thus we are presented with what 'Rabbi' John Duncan called a trilemma – Jesus is mad, bad or God. Either He was trying to deceive people, or He was himself deluded, or He was stating the sober truth. This argument was developed by C. S. Lewis in *Mere Christianity*. In fact, people did say Jesus was mad; they said He had a demon, but they could not really explain away the fact that Jesus showed perfect love and perfect sanity and yet clearly said, 'I am the Son of God.' And this astonishing person, Jesus Christ, had this amazing love that He showed to the outcast, the downtrodden, the rejected – this love that broke through and still breaks through to us today.

Of course, there are those who say, as Richard Dawkins does, that there is another possibility: that Jesus claimed to be God, but He was mistaken. Some mistake! Why would a monotheistic Jew make such a mistake? It beggars belief.

I believe we are forced by logic and the evidence to the view that Jesus simply is who He claimed to be – the unique Son of God.

But why would God become man? Anselm, the Archbishop of Canterbury around A.D. 1100, wrote a book *Cur Deus Homo?* (*Why did God become Man?*). In it he shows that man had to render satisfaction to God for his sin, but that only God Himself could adequately make amends. Therefore, for our salvation we needed the incarnation. Only Jesus the God-Man could deal with our alienation from God.

That's why God became man: to pay the price of our sin. This is not an intellectual game. It is about reconciliation to God – peace with God – freely offered to us in the gospel.

Supremely, I have come to know God's existence and His love in the death of Jesus Christ. Jesus said quite clearly that He had not come just to live, or to preach; He came to die: 'For even the Son of

Man did not come to be served but to serve, and to give his life as a ransom for many' (Mark 10:45); and that is what He did in dying on the cross. The answer to all our questions about God is right there at the cross, the very centre of all history, where Jesus died for our sins.

But what's the proof of all this? Interestingly enough, the apostle Paul used just that word 'proof' of Jesus rising from the dead (Acts 17:31).

Historian Michael Grant states: 'the historian ... cannot justifiably deny the empty tomb' because normally applied historical criteria indicate that, 'the evidence is firm and plausible enough to necessitate the conclusion that the tomb was indeed found empty.'[18] Now that is not the same as saying that Jesus rose from the dead. However, it highlights the point that all who study the story of Jesus seriously have to account for the empty tomb. Many who have done so have been persuaded by the evidence that Jesus in fact did so rise.

Journalist Frank Morison set out to write a book about Jesus that would disprove the resurrection, because he felt it spoiled the real heroic story of Jesus' life. However, when he came to write his book (*Who Moved the Stone?*) after investigation of the evidence, his first chapter was entitled, 'The book that refused to be written.' He became convinced that the only satisfactory explanation of the evidence was that Jesus did rise from the dead.

Lord Darling (a former Lord Chief Justice) said of the resurrection: 'In its favour as a living truth there exists such overwhelming evidence, positive and negative, factual and circumstantial, that no intelligent jury in the world could fail to bring in the verdict that the resurrection story is true.'[19]

For these and many other reasons, I am not an atheist. I believe that God exists. I am not an atheist, because I believe there is ample evidence that God exists and, supremely, that God is love. I know that my Redeemer lives (Job 19:25), because I know the Son of God who loved me and gave Himself for me (Gal. 2:20).

---

18 Michael Grant, *Jesus: An Historian's Review of the Gospels* (Charles Scribner's Sons, 1977), p. 176.

19 Quoted by Michael Green in *Man Alive* (London: InterVarsity Fellowship, 1967), p. 53f.

And I am convinced that there is good evidence for you too to believe – not only that God exists, but that He loves you and has done everything necessary to establish a living and eternal relationship with you.

6

A PSYCHIATRIST
explains why he is not an Atheist

PABLO MARTINEZ

The French thinker Foucault observed that in too many debates the protagonists regard their opponent as an enemy to be defeated. This is precisely the kind of attitude I wish to avoid in the reflections which follow. They are drawn from my own personal experience; this is why I write from a position of respect towards those who think differently, especially those who define themselves as atheists. We are all constantly learning and we should have the necessary humility to recognize our limitations. Disagreeing with each other's *ideas* shouldn't imply a rejection of each other as *persons*.

My aim in this chapter is not to defeat an opponent but rather to enrich and, if possible, to open the eyes to faith of those who don't have it. My faith is the most important treasure in my life and I wish to share this 'pearl of great value' (Matt. 13:46) in the spirit and the words of Teresa of Avila: 'If you have God, what do you lack? If you lack God, what do you have?'

PART ONE: FIVE SHORTAGES WHICH LEAVE A VOID

I have chosen five reasons why I am not an atheist. I could mention others, but these are the most important in the development of my faith. I begin with the emotional and existential reason – an area where subjectivism abounds – because it is the area with which I am

93

most familiar as a practicing psychiatrist and because it is that which allows me to develop the theme from the perspective requested: my personal experience. Faith has an irreplaceably subjective element. To believe is not only a question of debating arguments or reasons like those who play a game of chess that is won or lost according to the forcefulness of the arguments or the skill of the player. Belief certainly involves one's reason but, ultimately, it is a question of the heart. That is why Pascal, in one of his most brilliant thoughts, said that the heart has its reasons that reason doesn't understand.

I am not an atheist for these reasons:

1. Atheism doesn't fill the deepest human needs: it is existentially frustrating

Infelicissimus – profoundly unhappy – this is what the philosopher Herbert H. Spencer asked to be inscribed on his tombstone. Scientific materialism occupied a primary place for this British thinker and, judging by his sad epitaph, the atheism of his philosophy did not satisfy the very deepest needs of his being. The final balance of his life was in no way very agreeable. In the face of death, doubts were not stilled and sincerity surfaced: he was 'profoundly unhappy'.

All human beings ask certain essential questions whose answers constitute the basis of their existence. They are the columns which support their existential and emotional well-being because they give significance to life and provide happiness and peace. People feel happy when their life has meaning and very unhappy when they have to admit, 'I don't know what I'm doing here; my life is absurd.'

In my experience, the authentic significance of human life is inseparably bound up with God. In God I found the true meaning of life. On the other hand, I believe atheism produces frustration because it doesn't provide satisfactory answers to three basic questions about life which reflect the most profound human needs:

• Who am I? Where have I come from? The need for identity.

• What is life? Why am I here? The need for purpose.

• What is there after death? Where do I go? The need for hope.

Without God, the answer is that of the wise preacher in the Book of Ecclesiastes, possibly the first existentialist treatise in history: 'Vanity of vanities, all is vanity ... So I hated life, for the work which had been done under the sun was grievous to me, because everything is futility and striving after the wind' (Eccles. 1:2; 2:17, NASB).

When you honestly contemplate life and death outside God, frustration – a feeling of emptiness and absurdity – is the most likely conclusion. Life becomes meaningless because atheism is a discourse without hope. The French thinker Edgar Morin put it this way: 'We feel perplexed and disorientated in our situation in the world since we have known that we find ourselves in a little spinning top that travels round a ball of fire in space.'[1]

In the final analysis, nothing fills this vacuum outside of God: neither work, nor study, nor pleasure, nor riches are able to provide the ultimate meaning to human existence. All these things may mitigate the thirst for meaning but they are really just 'existential aspirins' which only calm the malaise for a while. Once their effect has passed, frustration and a sense of emptiness reappear with still greater force.

This was the case with George Eastman, inventor of the commerical camera and founder of the famous company Kodak. Considered one of the most generous philanthropists in America, he donated half his fortune to charitable works, but it seemed that nothing could fill his life. Already old, he committed suicide at the age of 78. Is it mere coincidence that some of the wealthiest and most famous men have ended their days taking their own lives? In such a materialist world which worships the money god, we need to bear in mind that material goods and possessions can be a legitimate and excellent *means* but not an *end* in themselves because they cannot provide any meaning for existence.

This void in our lives can manifest itself in many ways, but I would like to single out two: existential anxiety and our attitude towards death.

---

1   Quoted by Juan Insua in the Spanish newspaper *La Vanguardia* (Barcelona, 23 July 1985), p. 30. He refers to Edgar Morin´s book *Para salir del siglo XX* (Getting out of the XX Century), Editorial Kairos.

One of the deepest causes of anxiety is the lack of purpose in life. This is what we call existential anxiety. This condition is not due to any biochemical disturbance of the brain; it springs from man's central problem: the absence of meaning in life with its inevitable results – desperation and the sense of cosmic disorientation. It is a disturbing inner unrest that goes far beyond the symptoms of clinical anxiety and it is not relieved by drugs or by psychotherapy because it is ultimately a spiritual/existential problem.

Carl Jung, the Swiss psychiatrist, emphasizing the existential origin of neuroses, wrote: 'Meaninglessness inhibits fullness of life and is therefore equivalent to illness. Meaning makes a great many things endurable, perhaps everything.'[2]

Existential anxiety is certainly ameliorated by finding enriching relationships. Significant relationships may become a soothing instrument, but they are not enough. Human relationships need to be of two dimensions: with our fellow human beings, but also with our Creator. Such was man's original condition. It is in this sense that the atheist world view, with its subsequent separation from God, is the ultimate source of anxiety because it prevents our deepest need from being met.

Another example of this deep malaise outside of God can be seen in our attitude to death. As a psychiatrist, I have been a privileged witness of the great difference in the way believers and non-believers face death. The former face it calmly and peacefully; those who have no faith approach the end with much more unease, at times charged with irony or cynicism.

The lack of hope is, above all, the main weakness of atheism. A world without God is a world without hope, a desert which, sooner or later, leads to pessimism and scepticism.

Aren't these the distinctive characteristics of contemporary Europe? The philosophy of life of our postmodern society is an accurate reflection of its fundamental scepticism: 'It's not worth thinking about the future because I don't know what the future holds.' The absence of a solid hope is like a venom which ends up

---

2   C. G. Jung, *Memories, Dreams, Reflections* (Collins, Fontana Library, 1972), p. 373.

poisoning all the areas of life. When you look at life face-to-face without masks, atheism – with its despair – leads to desperation. Such was the experience of an illustrious atheist like Jean-Paul Sartre in his book *Nausea* when he affirmed in a fit of personal openness: 'Nausea has not left me and I do not think it will leave me so soon ... I myself am nausea.'[3]

Hope is the indispensable antidote to frustration. In the words of the Protestant theologian, Emil Brunner: 'What oxygen is to the lungs, such is hope to the meaning of life.'[4] Without oxygen, we die of asphyxia. Without hope, we suffer from the suffocating effects of despair with its sense of emptiness, of the sheer absurdity of life.

Only hope can give meaning to life and throw light on the darkest corners of our existence. Lack of hope is death in life itself. However, the essential question is *what do we hope for?* – or, better still, *in whom do we hope? Does our hope have some foundation?*

In my experience, faith lifts my eyes up to see higher and further to where I find *the God of all hope* (Rom. 15:13). It's my innermost conviction that atheism could never carry me to these heights because it cannot provide a 'firm and secure hope' (an expression used in the Epistle to the Hebrews 6:19).

Man has needs, longings and a sense of disquiet in the deepest parts of his being which transcend the purely material and temporal; it is a thirst for eternity, a thirst for transcendence that is not satisfied by any human experience. It can be disguised or concealed, it can be repressed, but it erupts time and again. The English writer C. S. Lewis put it this way: 'If I find in myself a desire which no experience in this world can satisfy, the most probable explanation is that I was made for another world.'[5]

Why does atheism not respond to the great enigmas of existence and thus become frustrating? The answer will take us to the next argument.

---

3   J-P. Sartre, *La Nausée* (Buenos Aires, Losada, 1947), p. 144 published in English as *Nausea* (London: Penguin Modern Classics, 2000).

4   Quoted by A. Scioli and H. Biller, *Hope in the age of anxiety* (Oxford University Press, 2009), p. 346.

5   C. S. Lewis, *Mere Christianity* (Collins, Fontana Books, 1972), p. 118.

2. Atheism reduces a human being to genes and cells: it is anthropologically materialistic

'We play from strength and our strength is science and technology ... we need to make vast changes to human behavior ... What we need is a technology of behavior ... [this is] the only way to solve our problems.'[6] These words by the renowned psychologist B. F. Skinner sum up the basic point of many atheist thinkers today and reflect one of their essential premises: scientific materialism. Their anthropology (view of man) is profoundly materialistic. The human being is, quite simply, the most developed animal. He is the most highly evolved being in the zoological scale, having reached the crest after a long process of natural selection. Man is something like 'a monkey with clothes'.

We are just genes and cells. Our brain functioning is no more than biochemical reactions. No place for the old-fashioned ideas of the soul or the spirit. These are 'myths that need to be buried'. In *The DNA Mystique,* the authors analyze this growing fascination with what could be called 'the gene culture'[7] and accurately explain how our genetic code is little by little becoming a powerful, even magical, entity that governs everything in our lives.

The place that previously was given to God – as the ultimate being responsible for our destiny – is now given to our genes. Many people today believe that the genetic code will eventually account for absolutely every aspect of human behaviour. In this sense, genetic determinism becomes a sort of religion where the 'myth of the DNA' may easily be the promoter of a new value scale.

This argument applied to the brain has made neurosciences very popular today. It pretends to explain religious phenomena in the following way: faith and religion are nothing more than responses of the brain to specific stimuli. The same thing occurs with other emotions: happiness, aggressiveness, and others. It is not

---

6   B. F. Skinner, *Beyond Freedom and Dignity*, (New York: Bantam/Vintage, 1972), pp. 1-3, 23.

7   D. Nelkin & S. Lindee, *The DNA Mystique: The Gene as a Cultural Icon* (New York: W.H. Freeman and Company, 1995).

yet known what specific area of the cerebral hemisphere or of our genes corresponds to religious propensity, but this is only a matter of time. In the same way that many kinds of social behaviour – alcoholism, gambling, violent traits and even adultery – are explained and justified because they are supposedly 'written in our genes', religion is just a conditioned response having to do with the biochemistry of our brain.

According to the materialistic way of thinking, faith would not be anything more than the elaborate expression of a sophisticated instinct – the religious impulse – of the most developed animal. It is not related to an objective reality, God, but it all happens inside us.

This is not the proper place to respond to this argument from a scientific viewpoint. Let me just give an illustration to demonstrate my opinion in this regard. When a young man is in love with his girlfriend, a series of biochemical changes takes place in his brain. His adrenaline increases and endorphins are released. A correct laboratory analysis would provide us with the experimental evidence of these alterations. But no one would say that the young man was in love because his endorphins had increased! The biochemical processes do not subtract from the reality of his love for her; they do not deny or affirm his being in love. Nor do they tell us anything about the existence or about the perfection of his girlfriend. Why? The experimental description of a phenomenon neither denies nor proves anything about the truth of this phenomenon. It simply describes a mechanism and mechanisms never explain the *why*, but only the *how*.

It is my conviction that another kind of immaterial reality does exist; we cannot perceive it, though, because our senses are not properly equipped to do so. Nonetheless, this doesn't exclude its existence. The French writer Antoine de Saint-Exupery wrote: 'One sees clearly only with the heart; what is essential is invisible to the eyes.'[8] We cannot be so arrogant as to affirm that the only things that exist are those within the reach of our sensorial perception

---

8   Antoine de Saint-Exupery, *El principito* (*The Little Prince*) (Buenos Aires: Alianza Emecé Editores, 1984), p. 87.

capacity. As Jung said: 'It is almost a ridiculous prejudice to suppose that existence can only be corporeal.'[9] Many realities exist that we cannot perceive because we are finite beings. Obviously, one of these greater realities is God; if God exists, He is spirit (as Jesus Himself stated) and therefore He cannot be found through material tools or experimental methods. This idea leads to my third reason.

3. Atheism seeks the truth by one path alone: it is methodologically reductionist

'The great error of the modern world has been to consider that what can't be heard, touched or seen is an illusion. Basic reality is not directly observable.'[10]

When you have such a materialistic view of man, the only source of knowledge is science. The truth of things is not sought through reflection, but in the experimental knowledge of how and why they are produced. This is the logical outcome of a materialistic anthropology: if we are nothing more than a cluster of genes and cells, then those means of acquiring knowledge which lead us to seek a spiritual dimension are superfluous.

The only way to understand the reality of life and of human beings is to apply 'scientific criteria', criteria that follow the fashionable paradigm which today happens to be the computer model applied to the brain. With evident complacency, a Spanish journalist wrote: 'Scientific advances result in constant reductions in the field of ethical and philosophical speculation. Science – especially neuroscience – is consistently throwing more and more light ... Very popular myths, such as the inherent nature of human violence, have to be buried because science is proving they are wrong.'[11] Observe how this 'scientific' approach is applied to an issue which is plainly anthropological and sociological – violence – whose origins are sought in the brain. No place for anything else.

---

9   C. G. Jung, *Psicología y Religión* (Barcelona: Paidos, 1981), p. 2.

10   Interview with Ervin Laszlo, *La Vanguardia* (Barcelona, August 16, 2012), p. 48. Laszlo is a contemporary scientific specialist in the Philosophy of Science.

11   Pedro Vallín, *The Role of Contemporary Thinkers* (*La Vanguardia*, August 15, 2012), pp. 24-5.

In contrast, here is the attitude of one of the most lucid minds, Albert Einstein: 'My religion consists of a humble admiration of the illimitable superior spirit who reveals himself in the slight details we are able to perceive with our frail and feeble mind. That deeply emotional conviction of the presence of a superior reasoning power, which is revealed in the incomprehensible universe, forms my idea of God.'[12]

Einstein reminds us here of an important principle: emotion and reason are two ways to valid knowledge and are not necessarily mutually antagonistic. Einstein's 'deep emotional conviction', the 'heart' in Pascal's expression or 'the intuition' which Jung called 'the voice of the gods', have always been, and in all cultures, a form of knowledge. Actually, according to the latest investigations, the emotions have the same or greater weight in the brain than logic. However, intuitive thinking and reflection are disdained in our materialist society because the fashionable paradigm excludes the spiritual dimension of the human being. They hinder, thereby, the natural access to the profoundest aspects of life.

Reason needs to see in order to believe; faith believes in order to see. Their respective starting points are diametrically opposed because they both represent distinct facets of truth. Reason explores visible reality; intuition – and faith – is interested in that immaterial and invisible part which is unapproachable for scientific empiricism. Reason and science are not the only source of knowledge, though to accept this requires a certain degree of humility – the 'epistemological modesty' or 'intellectual humility' which Karl Popper mentions in some of his writings. According to this humility, science should display intellectual modesty.

A good friend of mine, a scientist himself, put it this way, 'Being a good scientist implies knowing what we don't know, that we know very little or that we never know all that we claim to know.'

Reality, said the philosopher Hegel, is a prism with many facets. We cannot seek it nor understand it by looking at one facet only. All experimental and scientific explanations are no more than a small

---

12   Quoted by Rob Kaplan, *Science Says* (New York: The Stonesong Press, 2001), p. 12.

area of knowledge. Categories of moral, spiritual and other kinds of knowledge exist that escape the measuring instruments of any scientist. This is because the object of science is not to judge the value of reality, but rather to discover what reality is like.

Let me quote Ernest Sabato, an Argentinian trained in the field of physical sciences. These excerpts (from his essay, *On the body, the soul and the total crisis of man*) are an excellent reminder of the danger of neglecting spiritual reality and the limitations of science:

> Modern man knows the forces that govern the external world and he puts them at his service; he's the god of the earth, his weapons are gold and intelligence; his methodology is reason and calculus; his objective is the universe. The first cause doesn't interest these engineers. Technical knowledge takes the place of the metaphysical; efficiency and precision replace the metaphysical concerns ...
>
> The attempt to demonstrate the passing of the 'primitive' mentality to the 'positive' consciousness will conclude three decades later with the pathetic confession of its defeat, when the wise will finally have to recognize that such a primitive, or pre-logical mentality, doesn't exist as an inferior stage of man, but that both planes co-exist in any time period and culture.[13]

4. Atheism makes a god of man: it is morally egocentrical

'If God doesn't exist, then I am God.'[14] Atheism raises man to the category of God, it deifies him. Perhaps we have here one of the main reasons why human beings have always wanted to 'kill God'. The idea of the death of God didn't originate with Nietzsche but rather goes back to the origins of the human race: 'You will be like God' was the original temptation of the devil (Gen. 3:5). The longing to convert oneself into a 'little god' has been an irresistible temptation throughout the history of humanity.

---

13   E. Sabato, *Sobre el Cuerpo, el Alma y la Crisis Total del Hombre*. Exclusive essay written for *Tribuna Médica*, nos. 588 & 589, December 1974.

14   F. Dostoyevsky, *The Brothers Karamazov*.

It is a curious paradox: on the one hand, atheism reduces man to a machine of conditioned reflexes, only genes and cells, the most evolved animal in creation. On the other hand, it makes him feel like God. How is this apparently contradictory phenomenon produced? Atheism deifies because it displaces God, putting the human being in the centre. *The centre is me.* In its very essence, it is a morally egocentrical system.

Let's observe the logical correlation of facts: if God doesn't exist, then I am autonomous; no one can tell me how to live. At first sight, this seems like a respectable affirmation, morally inoffensive. But autonomy – *nobody over me* – leads inseparably to moral self-sufficiency: I am my own judge and guide, I don't have to give account to anybody. Self-sufficiency leads finally to self-realization, the right to fulfill my real self with little – if any – concern for the price others may have to pay. When God disappears from the horizon, truth and ethics become subjective – it's a question of personal opinions – and private interests prevail over those of the community.

Atheism – with its autonomous ethics – is inseparable from an egotistical worldview of life. As some atheist thinkers recognize, it is really difficult to elaborate an ethics centred on love from an atheistic perspective and it is much more difficult still to live it. No wonder when the limits between truth and error, good and bad, become totally blurred because they are subjective.

Furthermore, egocentrism usually goes hand in hand with narcissism: love directed at oneself. We live in a narcissistic society and there are more and more 'men who are lovers of themselves' (in the language of the apostle Paul – 2 Timothy 3:2), a clearly visible tendency, for example, in modern psychology where 'the cult of self-worship' is a prominent feature.

Of course, there are atheists who abound in goodness and altruism, excellent people who have made significant contributions to society. We mustn't fall into the trap of simplistic dualism: everything is good in the believer and everything is bad in the atheist. The divine image – *imago dei* – is inherent, albeit stained and damaged, in every human being and the 'common grace' of God continues to reach all, believers and unbelievers alike. For God, each person has immense value *per se,* regardless of their beliefs.

This, however, does not mitigate the reality: the further people distance themselves from God, the more they become their own god with all the moral, existential and social implications of this alienation. The myth of Narcissus reminds us how falling in love with oneself – the consequence of egocentrism – ends in tragedy. Let us see it.

5. Atheism generates fragility in relationships: it is socially individualistic

Erich Fromm, American thinker and psychoanalyst, expounds in his work the idea that the death of God was the problem of the nineteenth century, but in the twentieth century the problem was the death of man. Unfortunately, Fromm saw no connection between the two facts.

The 'death of God' leads sooner or later to the 'death of man' as we saw in the myth of Narcissus, who ended up overwhelmingly dominated by his self-love. Why are both facts related? Self-deification, with its accompanying entourage of egoism and narcissism, leads to sheer individualism. The more people eliminate God and become the centre of their lives, the more their rights and their needs are enhanced. Eventually individualism produces a profound erosion of relationships, which become fragile and superficial. This way the 'death of God' ends up generating a profound social malaise that we can rightly compare to 'the death of man'.

It is no coincidence that the rampant process of secularization in the West has been accompanied by rising individualism. When the self is the axis around which my life revolves, it becomes easy to arrive at the attitude 'I only want what I need' (the god pragmatism). Principles are subordinated to 'my needs' and 'my convenience', dispensing with everything that is not useful to me. So, for many people today, being happy is equivalent to 'being myself', regardless of the cost to others. 'I need to be myself' is the more or less elegant cloak that conceals exacerbated individualism.

Let's look at two examples of this link between 'the death of God' and its accompanying social malaise.

We are witnessing today a colossal crisis of fidelity. I am referring not only to conjugal fidelity but to all human relationships (parents and children, siblings, friends, etc.). Many emotional and social problems arise from the instability of the relationships, the fragility of the bonds. What sociologists call 'social instability' conceals a crisis of fidelity where the deep-rooted links that used to be for life have now become precarious and with a very early 'expiry date'. The slogan today seems to be 'nothing long-term'.

With this erosion of commitment, an important source of security and personal identity has been lost. Obviously this has its price, a price we are paying in the shape of an epidemic of broken relationships with its accompanying retinue: emotional problems, particularly anxiety, depression and loneliness.

A second example is aggressiveness. Individualism generates and – at the same time is nourished by – aggressiveness in a kind of ill-fated feedback. Thus we see a rising number of suicides – aggressiveness directed at oneself – and of murders, such as the recent indiscriminate massacres of children and adolescents by gun-carrying killers. Aggressiveness also manifests itself in much more subtle ways, some of which are even approved by a hypercompetitive society. The world of business experiences situations every day in which the 'me' is asserted in an almost Darwinian fashion: in order to get on, everything is permissible. It doesn't matter that I have to trample on or mistreat my colleagues. How many meteoric careers have left a trail of emotional 'corpses' in their wake?!

The problem is complex and we can't simplify it. The moral and spiritual malaise of our society is a many-sided phenomenon in which different kinds of factors intervene. However, one needn't be a psychiatrist to recognize that behind many conflicts in daily life there lurks a history of people abounding in tedium, resentment against life, or a simple sense of absurdity. What ends up being a social drama was originally a personal and existential drama.

Atheism is incapable of generating a strong sense of community, unlike religions in general and Christianity in particular. The recent declarations of the founder of the first atheist church in London, 'The Nave', attracted my attention: 'We believe it would be a shame not to enjoy the same things as religion, like a sense of community.'[15]

Is it possible to have a strong sense of community with an atheist world view? In the light of what we have considered so far, the answer is 'No' – at least not with the solidity and intensity of the believer. Concern for one's neighbour is an essential part of Christian ethics to such an extent that even non-Christian thinkers recognize that the most singular contribution of Christianity to Western civilization is the ethic of love. Loving your neighbour, with its strong sense of community, is the natural result of God's love. It can be no other way when the moral demand *par excellence* made of the Christian is 'Love God above all things and your neighbour as yourself' (cf Mark 12:30-31).

PART TWO: THREE PIECES OF EVIDENCE THAT MAKE ONE THINK

1. Man may kill God but he cannot stifle the thirst for God

'I don't believe in God, but I miss him.'[16]

With this striking sentence, Julian Barnes begins his autobiography. The experience of the English writer reflects that of millions of people, just as the Psalmist expressed in another famous quote: 'As the deer pants for the water brooks, so my soul thirsts for God, for the living God' (Ps. 42:1-2, NASB).

Man can proclaim the death of God, as Nietzsche did, but he cannot eliminate the *thirst for God,* which becomes distorted or repressed, giving place to the 'new faiths' and to secular gods before which he kneels. The churches are emptying, but the sports stadiums, cinemas and fashion parades are the temples where the new gods are worshipped with the fervour and devotion appropriate

---

15   Sanderson Jones, quoted by the *Huffington Post UK*, January 8, 2013.

16   Julian Barnes, *Nothing To Be Frightened Of.* Extract of his book quoted in *The Guardian*, Saturday, 23 February 2008.

to a religion. They are the contemporary forms of a spirituality without God.

The repression of God hasn't managed to make man a less religious being. The thirst for God – what the psychiatrist Viktor Frankl called 'unconscious religiosity'[17] – continues today, more alive than ever. Modern man pretends to be free of religious burdens and boasts of his secularism: 'we have liberated ourselves from the bonds of religion to live in real freedom.'

He fails to realize, however, that he has become a slave of the idols he has created. These are the secular gods he pays homage to and serves with as much passion as servility. Hedonism, relativism and pragmatism are some of the current secular gods. Time has proved the French thinker Paul Claudel right when he predicted many years ago that the twenty-first century would be religious or it would be nothing.

Atheistic spirituality, so popular today, is basically a self-made and hedonist 'menu'. No wonder when it is the fruit of a self-centred heart. It picks up 'a bit from everywhere' with one main goal: to contribute to the harmonic development of the self. Spirituality is an inner energy which you can cultivate and which makes you feel better with yourself and with others. The spiritual shouldn't be denied or repressed, but it should be relativized and reduced to the private sphere. Neither religion nor God is necessary.

The evidence seems to be obstinately clear, nevertheless, that dispensing with God does not result in the suppression of the need for God: the thirst for transcendence, which is nowadays temporarily quenched by any cheap substitute, remains intact. How right is the idea (attributed to the English thinker G. K. Chesterton) that when a man stops believing in God, he doesn't then believe in nothing, he believes anything.

---

17   Viktor Frankl develops this idea especially in his book *La Presencia Ignorada de Dios* (*The Unconscious God*) (Barcelona: Editorial Herder, 1991)

2. Believing in the materialist origin of the universe requires a lot of faith

'The possibility that the universe was formed by chance alone is equivalent to a hurricane entering a scrap heap and leaving a fully-formed aeroplane.'[18]

'Evolutionary mechanisms have made us humans after millions of years of mutations, errors, successes and selection.'[19]

The faith of an atheist requires, sincerely, an effort of credulity much greater than Christian faith. Isn't this faith in chance and this absolute confidence in evolutionary mechanisms much greater than faith in a creator God?

It doesn't occur to anyone to believe that a space vehicle is capable of rising into space, orbiting the earth and landing at a precise time and place without the careful work of numerous technicians and experts who have planned it all down to the minutest detail. We accept this as normal, but then we believe that the multitude of stars which move around the cosmos with rigorous precision appeared by the law of chance and necessity and that they have reached this perfection by 'spontaneous mutations'.

Quite honestly, it requires much more credulity – I hesitate to call it faith – to believe that the universe emerged from nothing and is sustained by laws born of chance than to believe in a creator God. In other words, I am not an atheist because for me it is much more logical to believe in causality than in coincidence.

For my part, I fully subscribe to the words of Alfred Kastler, who was awarded the Nobel Prize for Physics in 1966: 'The idea that the world, the material universe created itself seems absurd to me. I can only conceive of the world with a creator, therefore a God.'[20] Or in the words of Sir Isaac Newton: 'The marvelous

---

18   Sir Fred Hoyle, renowned cosmologist and physicist, quoted by Ervin Laszlo, *La Vanguardia,* August 16, 2012, p. 48.

19   Interview with Erwin Neher, *La Vanguardia*, January 15, 2010, p. 48. Neher was winner of the Nobel Prize for Medicine in 1991.

20   Quoted by José Jiménez Lozano, *Cartas de un cristiano impaciente* (Destino. Año 1968, n° 1614-1617, septiembre); editor Biblioteca de Catalunya.

construction of the universe with its incomparable harmony could only have been achieved according to the plans of an omniscient and all-powerful being.'[21]

3. Man rejects God without actually knowing Him

'I don't believe God exists, but if he exists, he has no pardon from God.'[22]

Which God has this man known for him to make such a bold declaration? What does he know about God to reach this conclusion? Unfortunately, there are many people like Sacristán; they reject a caricature of God but they have never known what the real God is like. They think they know Him but they have never discovered the character of the personal God revealed in the Bible. Without being aware of it, they make the same mistake that they accuse believers of, but exactly the reverse: they have created an image of God which is more the result of their frustrations and desires than the actual reality. (The problem of psychological projection can be found in the believer as much as in the atheist.)

As well as the atheist who is ignorant of the true God, there is another situation which occurs frequently: the person who is an atheist from reaction. Many people become atheists as a reaction to a hard, punishing, severe God, the product of a rigid, suffocating Christianity deprived of essential aspects of the Christian faith, such as mercy, grace and freedom. This was the case with Karl Marx, Ludwig Feuerbach, Sigmund Freud, Hermann Hesse and other famous atheists who were brought up in a very legalistic religious family environment and, in some cases, also studied in a seminary. The list of atheists 'from reaction' would be very long and it is very sad to realize how so many people have rejected God without having the correct knowledge of Him.

---

21   *La Buena Semilla* (*Daily devotional thoughts*) (Perroy, Switzerland: Ediciones Bíblicas La Buena Semilla, 18 January 2013).

22   Interview with José Sacristán, Spanish actor, *La Vanguardia,* January 14 2013, p. 48.

CONCLUSION: I AM NOT AN ATHEIST BECAUSE I HAVE BEEN CAPTIVATED BY THE PERSONAL GOD OF THE BIBLE

'I led them with cords of human kindness, with ties of love.' (Hosea 11:4)

'And I, if I be lifted up from the earth, will draw all men to Myself.' (Jesus in John 12:32, NASB).

The aim of this book is to explain 'why I am not an atheist.' However, I cannot finish at this point because it would not reflect the totality of my spiritual pilgrimage. There remains an argument which is the most important one. I have not only rejected atheism for its limitations and deficiencies but also for a positive reason: I have encountered the light which illuminates the darkness of life.

A whole book would be required to explain why I am a Christian. Therefore, I must limit myself to two brief reflections concerning my faith by way of conclusion.

WHAT IS MY GOD LIKE?

In the first place, if I have become a Christian it is because I have come to know a God who has attracted me in an irresistible way; in the words of the prophet Jeremiah, a God who has 'persuaded me' (Jer. 20:7). I discovered that God did not force me to believe, but put in me the desire to know Him and to love Him. My God is practically the opposite of the one many atheists reject:

- He is not a God of fear but of love;

- He is not a repressive God but 'slow to anger, abounding in love' (Ps. 103:8);

- He is not a God of capricious tyranny but of precious freedom;

- He is a God close to me whom I can know not only with the head but love with the heart;

- He is a God who delights in being called 'Father';

- He is a God who, though being Almighty, suffers with me and is at my side in my afflictions;

110

- He is a God who, though being absolute Truth, delights in persuading rather than imposing;

- He is a God of mysteries and enigmas – the hidden God – but also the God revealed in Jesus Christ, the image of the invisible God. Christ is the mirror of God; in His person and His life, He manifests without the slightest blemish the divine character.

This is the God that attracts me. I can say of Him like the Psalmist: 'For with you is the fountain of life; in your light we see light' and 'How priceless is your unfailing love, O God! People take refuge in the shadow of your wings' (Ps. 36:9 &7).

'THE HIDDEN ROOM AND THE GOD-SHAPED VOID'

In the second and final place, I am not an atheist because I have found in Jesus Christ the fullest sense of life here and now, and a firm hope for the life to come. From my own experience, both personal and professional, I can witness that there is a deep 'hidden room' in our heart that no psychiatric expertise or human resource can reach. It is a room related to our meaning in life and to our thirst for eternity.

I have discovered that the ultimate answer to human frustration can only be found in the abundant life that faith in Jesus provides. 'I have come that they may have life and have it to the full.' (John 10:10) This phrase of Jesus, a formidable synthesis of the whole of the gospel, summarizes my experience of faith: in the face of the drama of a frustrated life in a frustrating world, there rises the radiant figure of Christ who opened the door to me of a new, magnificent, superior life – in a word, a life abounding in meaning and hope.

I make mine the words of Pascal who referred to the ultimate cause of human frustration with this memorable thought: 'There is a God-shaped vacuum in the heart of every man that cannot be filled by any created thing but only by God, the Creator made known through Jesus Christ.'[23]

This is the same Christ that said of Himself: 'Come to me all who are weary and heavy-laden and I will give you rest. ... learn from me ... and you shall find rest for your souls' (Matt. 11:28-29).

---

23   Blaise Pascal, *Pensées* (Genève: Edition Pierre Cailler, 1947), p. 248.

7

ANOTHER PASTOR
explains why he is not an Atheist

DAVID RANDALL

'Is that your own idea', Jesus asked Pontius Pilate, 'or did others talk to you about me?' (John 18:34) The Roman governor was trying to find out why Jesus had been brought before him and he thought he would put Jesus on the spot, so he came right out with it – 'Are you the king of the Jews?' Jesus would go on to say that His kingship was not a worldly kingship, but with this question *He* would put *Pilate* on the spot.

The question might be put to us all – believers, agnostics, atheists or whatever we are: is our faith our own or are we simply accepting what others have told us?

Further, how do I respond to the challenge which people might put to someone like me: 'You only believe in Christianity because that's the way you were brought up'?

First of all, I would say that I am thankful that I was indeed brought up within the community of faith. Church was part of my life from my earliest days. I was baptized at seven weeks old, attended Sunday School, went to Scripture Union at school, and in every way was encouraged to develop a Christian understanding of reality and a Christian lifestyle.

But I am also thankful to be able to say that the acquired faith of my childhood has become my own. I can say what the Samaritans of John 4:42 said to the woman who had told them about Jesus: 'It is no longer because of what you said that we believe; for we have heard for ourselves, and we know that this is indeed the Saviour of the world' (ESV).

One's upbringing obviously does have a significant effect on what one becomes and I freely agree that my upbringing played a large part in making me what I am. However, the real issue is that of my own personal response to the message of Christianity and the person of Christ. I need, so far as possible, to stand back from the influences of my upbringing and consider my own response. This is what I have done at various points in my life. It has been necessary to consider my own response – to say (with the old song), it's not my mother or my father but it's me, O Lord, standing in the need of prayer.

It is interesting to reflect on the fact that many people, when they come to their teenage years especially, turn *against* the way they were brought up and reject the Christianity of their parents' generation. This is a common occurrence and, of course, a great disappointment to their believing parents and the church.

It works the other way too. There have been many instances of people who were not brought up to believe but they have become convinced believers in later years. Among such adult converts are thinkers such as C. S. Lewis, Alexander Solzhenitsyn and, more recently, the renowned scientist Francis Collins. Collins grew up as an agnostic and became a convinced atheist while studying for his Ph.D. in chemistry. Later, however, his outlook changed and in 2007 he wrote his *The Language of God*, subtitled, *A scientist presents evidence for belief*.[1]

The publisher's blurb on the back cover says: 'In *The Language of God* he explains his own journey from atheism to faith, and then takes the reader on a stunning tour of modern science to show that physics, chemistry and biology – indeed, reason itself – are not

---

1   Simon & Schuster (London, 2007).

incompatible with belief. His book is essential reading for anyone who wonders about the deepest questions of all: why are we here? How did we get here? And what does life mean?'

In the end, we all have to decide where we stand, whatever our background has been. If that background has been an atheistic one, people have to face the same issues: is your position your own, or is it just that others suggested it to you? Perhaps many unbelievers are such because that is the way *they* were brought up. This is the way in which many people are reared in today's secular culture (in the West, at any rate) and it might be said that they are biased towards atheism from the outset. The notion that Christianity is a Western religion and people believe it because they were brought up in 'a Christian country' can hardly be stated with integrity nowadays since we live in a Western world where it is counter-cultural to state that you are a convinced Christian and to stand against the anti-Christian pressures of contemporary political correctness which, as Melanie Phillips has graphically said, 'grips Western culture by the throat.'[2]

Alain de Botton faced that choice. He tells of his upbringing 'in a committedly atheistic household, as the son of two secular Jews who placed religious belief somewhere on a par with an attachment to Santa Claus', but in his mid-twenties he 'underwent a crisis of faithlessness' and had to work out his own position. He says that he never wavered in his certainty that God does not exist but was

> ... liberated by the thought that there might be a way to engage with religion without having to subscribe to its supernatural content ... I recognized that my continuing resistance to theories of an afterlife or of heavenly residents was no justification for giving up on the music, buildings, prayers, rituals, feasts, shrines, pilgrimages, communal meals and illuminated manuscripts of the faiths.[3]

He had to consider whether the atheism within which he had been nurtured was to be his own. Others of us have had to consider whether

---

2   In *The World Turned Upside Down* (Encounter, 2010), p. 289.

3   Alain de Botton, *Religion for Atheists* (Hamish Hamilton, 2012), p. 13.

the faith passed on to us is to be our own. If Socrates was correct in his assertion that the unexamined life is not worth living, then, whether we have been brought up to believe or disbelieve in any divine Being, we need to make up our own minds where we stand.

And we all do stand somewhere! Those who knowingly say that believers only believe because they were brought up to believe sometimes imply that they themselves stand in some position of detached neutrality and are therefore equipped to pass judgment on the belief or unbelief of others. But they themselves have a world view, a philosophy, a faith.

This is recognized by the writer of *Atheism* in the *Very Short Introduction* series of books. The author describes it as a book for atheists looking for a systematic defence and explanation of their position. He wrote: 'The guiding idea has been to produce a book which atheists will be able to give to their friends by way of explanation *for their beliefs* [my italics], after having used it themselves to help organise their thoughts.'[4] That comment accepts the fact that atheism is a faith position. Often today we hear talk about people 'of all faiths and none' – but who on earth are these people of no faith? Perhaps the reference is to people who are not members of any church or adherents of any organized religion, but the basic question is not *whether* people have faith but *in what* they have faith.

Christians have faith in a good and gracious God who makes Himself known in the works of a Maker's hand, in the 'eternity in the hearts' of human beings (Eccles. 3:11) and particularly in the life, death and resurrection of His Son, Jesus Christ. Others have a different faith, but it is a faith nonetheless. Consider some of its features:

- it is the faith to believe that this universe of order and beauty is the chance product of impersonal forces

- it is the faith that death is a terminus and there is nothing beyond, or perhaps the sentimental (placebo-like?) notion that,

---

4   Julian Baggini, *Atheism* (OUP, 2003), preface.

after this life is past, everyone ends up in some kind of 'happy land'

- it is faith to think (in the teeth of all the evidence) that human effort alone is going to build a better society

- it is faith to believe that many of the best brains there have ever been have been completely deluded in their faith in an unseen Divinity

- it is faith to believe that ever-increasing prosperity and possessions can lead to an inward sense of purpose and satisfaction

- it is faith to believe that our society can survive the loss of faith in God

These are items of faith, and the question is whether they are better-founded than the faith held by Christians in the God who, we believe, has made Himself known to us – supremely in and through Jesus Christ. Some may not profess any religion or belong to any church, but let's not come away with this nonsense about people of all faiths and none.

Having argued that I am not a Christian simply because of my upbringing, let me go on now to point to seven reasons why I am not an atheist – some negative (about the inadequacies of atheism) and some positive (about the adequacy of Christianity, or of Christ).

1. I am not an atheist because human experience points to the reality of God

Atheism flies in the face of almost universal human experience. The present decline of religious affiliation in European society is historically unusual, to say the least. In generation after generation in most cultures of the world, people have recognized that there is something beyond the realm of ordinary physical existence. It's what Augustine meant when he wrote that God has made us for Himself and our hearts are restless until they find their rest in Him.[5]

---

5   *Confessions of St Augustine*, Book 1 (Fontana Books, 1965), p. 31.

The writer of the Old Testament book of Ecclesiastes gave expression to it in the circumstances of his time: 'I built houses for myself and planted vineyards. I made gardens and parks and planted all kinds of fruit trees in them. I made reservoirs to water groves of flourishing trees. I bought male and female slaves and had other slaves who were born in my house. I also owned more herds and flocks than anyone in Jerusalem before me. I amassed silver and gold for myself.' He had everything, and yet, looking back on it all, he can say: 'Yet when I surveyed all that my hands had done and what I had toiled to achieve, everything was meaningless, a chasing after the wind; nothing was gained under the sun' (Eccles. 2:4-8a and 11). That phrase 'under the sun' is a recurring and significant phrase in Ecclesiastes. It stands for the materialistic outlook of those who put all their eggs in the basket of this-worldly success but find that there is still something lacking.

There is a spiritual thirst in the human heart. This may not prove the truth of Christianity, but it is strong evidence against atheism. If there is no God, whence comes this hunger?

2. I am not an atheist because of the world around us

This is another reason why I am not an atheist. Whether one looks at the immensities of space or the beauty of a butterfly, it strains credulity to think that such design has no Designer. The beauty and order of creation tell against atheism. As the believer replied to a French revolutionary who said they intended to tear down all memory of God, 'You won't be able to tear down the stars.' Atheism asks us to believe that there is no Designer behind the grandeur of creation and that there is no ultimate purpose in our existence.

Lord Russell was asked what he would say if he found out after dying that there is a God after all. He said that he would tell God that He hadn't given him enough evidence.[6] This is in direct conflict with the biblical teaching, expressed plainly in Romans 1:19-20: 'What may be known about God is plain to them. For since the

---

6   Quoted by A. J. Ayer, *Bertrand Russell* (University of Chicago Press, 1988), p. 131.

creation of the world God's invisible qualities – his eternal power and divine nature – have been clearly seen, being understood from what has been made, so that men are without excuse.' The previous verse says that the problem is that, although God has given ample evidence of His existence and glory, human beings have 'suppressed' that truth.

3. I am not an atheist because atheism smacks of wishful thinking

The enemies of Christianity are fond of accusing believers of indulging in wishful thinking about the purpose of our existence, the forgiveness of our sins and our hope of heaven, but what if they are the ones who are indulging in wishful thinking. They desperately *hope* that this life is all there is, that death is a terminus and there is no God with whom they have an unavoidable rendezvous.

As noted earlier in this book, Aldous Huxley was honest enough to admit as much. 'For myself', he wrote, 'as, no doubt, for most of my contemporaries, the philosophy of meaninglessness was essentially an instrument of liberation. The liberation we desired was simultaneously liberation from a certain political and economic system and liberation from a certain system of morality. We objected to the morality because it interfered with our sexual freedom... there was one admirably simple method of confuting these people and at the same time justifying ourselves in our political and erotic revolt: we could deny that the world had any meaning whatsoever.'[7]

Those who imagine that Christians are indulging in wishful thinking might well consider their own position. It is well known that Sigmund Freud suggested that religion is, at root, the comforting illusion that there is a father figure in heaven. What if it is the other way round? What if atheism is, at root, the comforting illusion that there is no Father in heaven so that we can do what we like and get away with it.

---

7   Aldous Huxley, *Ends and Means* (London: Chatto & Windus, 1937), p. 273. See also
     p. 75 of this book.

During the latter part of 2012, British society was shocked by the revelation that the late entertainer Jimmy Savile had been guilty of numerous instances of sexual abuse. People have been mystified about the fact that he kept it all secret and that it only came to light after his death. Are we simply to conclude that there is no justice anywhere and that he 'got away with it'? It does not constitute an argument for the existence of a God to whom we must all give account (Heb. 4:13), but we might consider whether the thought that death is a terminus is little more than a comforting illusion for those who would rather not answer for their deeds (and misdeeds).

The one-time Principal of Aberdeen University reflected on the eagerness with which we 'clutch at these explanations (Oedipus complex, etc) which explain away our sense of responsibility! This is why atheism has a perennial appeal; it is wishful thinking in its most enticing form.'[8]

4. I am not an atheist because of the fruits of atheism

Another of the charges that are often laid against religion in general and Christianity in particular is that many terrible things have been done in the name of religion. Critics of Christianity conveniently overlook the enormously beneficial effects of Christianity (notably in education and healthcare, so often the twin accompaniments of the advent of Christianity) and refer rather to the Crusades, the Inquisition and other acts of violence and repression carried out ostensibly in the name of Christ. In a recent television drama, a character referred to someone who was burned at the stake in the context of religious wars, and the enigmatic comment was heard, 'God save us from religion'!

Leaving aside the question of atheism's rationale for assessing what is good and what is evil, we can say that such things represent a misunderstanding (to say the least) of real Christianity. But what about the fruits of atheism? Another reason why I am not an atheist is the consideration of its fruits. If religion has killed its thousands, atheism has killed its tens of thousands. Many have been

---

8   Thomas Taylor, *Where One Man Stands* (Saint Andrew Press, 1960), p. 24.

maltreated and martyred because of atheism, even in the hoped-for enlightenment of the last century or so.

A. N. Wilson, after referring to the writings of the unbelieving poet Algernon Charles Swinburne, wrote: 'Whatever song we choose to sing after the century of Lenin, Stalin, Hitler, Mussolini, Mao Tse-tung, Pol Pot, Franco, Ataturk, and politicians and scientists who pioneered nuclear bombs, it is not very likely to be Swinburne's "Glory to man in the highest! For Man is the master of things".'[9]

Other names could be added since these words were written, and, even if there is no point in listing the faults of atheism and religion in some competitive manner, it is true that atheism has a poor track record in terms of neighbourliness, compassion and love.

5. I am not an atheist because of the inadequacies of atheism
Atheism does not have the power to change lives or bring peace and joy; yet through faith people have found just these things, along with comfort and strength even in the most difficult of circumstances. The atheist's dismissal of the profound effects of faith as psychological delusion simply doesn't stack up. I recall the story of an atheist standing in a mill complex telling the workers that religion is rubbish, when an uneducated mill-worker interrupted to say that until recently he had been a curse to himself, his family and everybody who knew him. Then he heard the gospel, opened his heart to Jesus and from that time on was a changed man, living a totally new life. He asked – if the Bible is false, what had happened in him? The atheist had no answer.

While many unbelievers seem to live contented and happy lives, it is also true that in the long term atheism does not change lives. It is the power of God that can change people and when we see the fruit of the Spirit (Gal. 5:22-23) it is evidence of the inner working

---

9   A. N. Wilson, *God's Funeral* (London: John Murray Ltd, 1999), p. 206. Wilson has turned his back on his earlier atheism, as explained in 'Why I Believe Again', published in *New Statesman*, 2 April 2009: http://www.newstatesman.com/religion/2009/04/conversion-experience-atheism (accessed 26 April 2013) See also *Why we should no longer be cowed by the chattering classes ruling Britain who sneer at Christianity*, published in *Daily Mail*, 11 April 2009 (accessed 26 April 2013).

of the Holy Spirit that can change self-centred people into people who put others first.

It is too simple to dismiss such change as merely a psychological quirk or emotional crisis. There may be times when people have been moved and perhaps even manipulated into some kind of dramatic change, but the instances of real, radical and lasting change are too many and too varied to dismiss in such a manner. Many have experienced what the apostle Paul found when, through an encounter with the risen Christ, he became a new person altogether (2 Cor. 5:17). Atheism produces no such radical and lasting change.

Also, atheism has no basis for morality. The point is argued elsewhere in this volume. If there is no ultimate Power, then there is no basis for morality. Even Nietzsche realized this; he wrote: 'When one gives up the Christian faith, one pulls the right to Christian morality out from under one's feet. This morality is a system, a whole view of things thought out together. By breaking one main concept out of it, the faith in God, one breaks the whole. It stands or falls with faith in God.'[10]

Many have been the efforts to find a basis for morality apart from any religious considerations, whether people seek to invent a new golden rule, bank on some kind of categorical imperative or simply rely on enlightened self-interest. The reality is that belief and behaviour, creed and conduct, go together; it is our beliefs that make us what we are.

This goes against the grain of contemporary culture in which it is held that beliefs don't matter. Beliefs do matter. Victor Frankl wrote about his grim experiences as an Austrian Jew who was imprisoned in concentration camps at Theresienstadt, Auschwitz and Dachau (his wife died at Bergen-Belsen, his father at Theresienstadt and his mother at Auschwitz). Reflecting on the horrors and barbarities of all that happened during that dreadful era, he wrote: 'When we present man as an automaton of reflexes, as a mind-machine, as a bundle of instincts, as a pawn of drives and reactions, as a mere

---

10   In *Twilight of the Idols* (1888), quoted by W. Storrar, *Scottish Identity* (Handsel Press, 1990), p. 181.

product of instinct, heredity and environment, we feed the nihilism to which modern man is, in any case prone.'[11]

He went on:

> I became acquainted with the last stage of that corruption in my second concentration camp, Auschwitz. The gas chambers of Auschwitz were the ultimate consequence of the theory that man is nothing but the product of heredity and environment ... I am absolutely convinced that the gas chambers of Auschwitz, Treblinka and Maidanek were ultimately prepared not in some Ministry or other in Berlin, but rather at the desks and in the lecture halls of nihilistic scientists and philosophers.

Of course, none of this is to be interpreted as suggesting that atheists are always or necessarily wicked people. To suggest such a thing would be absurd and we can and should applaud goodness, altruism and love wherever they are found. But we are still left with the question about the basis for moral judgments.

In Lord Russell's famous debate with Frederick Copleston, the latter asked Russell at one point whether he believed in right and wrong. When Russell said that he did, Copleston asked how Russell differentiated between the two. Russell replied that he distinguished them in the same way as he distinguished yellow from blue. When pressed, he was forced into stating that feeling was his guide.

The question might be posed in this manner: in the summer of 2011 there was rioting in some English cities. If one of the looters of shops had asked the question, 'Why shouldn't I take what I want?' what answer would be forthcoming? Put the emphasis on the word 'Why?' It is not 'Why *shouldn't* I?' but '*Why* shouldn't I?'

In Norway in the summer of 2011, a man killed 77 people in Oslo and on Utoeya Island. Right-minded people were appalled at this atrocity – but the uncomfortable question is, Why? Why are people appalled? Some may say it is self-evidently wrong to murder people, but (to press the issue) where does this 'self-evidently' come from? Atheism is hard pressed to give an answer

---

11   *The Doctor and the Soul* (Vintage, 1973), xxi, quoted by Ravi Zacharias, *The End of Reason* (Zondervan, 2008), p. 62f.

to this question. If there is no Law-Giver, no ultimate Authority, whence can come our moral judgements?

In British culture we still have many residual effects of Christian beliefs, even in the hearts and minds of many who have rejected the Christian creed. A phrase attributed to Ernest Renan described it as living on the perfume of an empty vase. The fragrance lingers for a while, but it will eventually fade. It is to be feared that this is what we find now, as time-honoured values are turned upside down. Western culture has cut itself off from its moorings (the authority of God) and is adrift on a sea of relativism without any chart or compass.

6. I am not an atheist because of the person and influence of Jesus Christ

Another reason that might be given for not embracing atheism (old or new) is that it does not account for the person and influence of Jesus Christ.

On atheist assumptions, it is difficult to account for the continuing impact of Jesus – His teaching, His influence, His life-changing power. His 'religion' ought to have faded away long ago! Many have predicted its demise and at present in the Western world many seem to think that Christianity is on the way out.

Yet there are many who maintain faith (cf. 1 Kings 19:18) and the reformer Theodore Beza's remark remains valid – that the church is an anvil that has worn out many a hammer. This is not because the church is a powerful and effective human organization, but because it is the church of the living God. If the church were a merely human institution, it would have died out long ago. It has been subjected to an enormous amount of attack, and today in this wild world strenuous efforts are being made in some countries to wipe Christianity out.[12] Yet, it survives. It survives because the church is the church of the living God. Atheism cannot account for this survival and growth of Christianity.

To take one crucial example, what can it make of belief in the resurrection of Jesus, the Easter message? Many books have gone

---

12   See e.g. http://www.barnabasfund.org/UK and http://www.csw.org.uk/home.htm.

in detail into the evidence for the resurrection of Christ[13] and here we merely refer briefly to this evidence.

At the time when stories were first circulating about Jesus having risen from the dead, many people had a vested interest in finding evidence to the contrary. So central to Christianity is the physical resurrection of Jesus that when Paul in Athens (Acts 17:18) spoke of Jesus and the resurrection (in Greek, *Jesus* and *anastasis*), some people thought he was referring to two gods (maybe a husband-and-wife team). But in these days the Jewish or Roman authorities could have quickly put paid to the growth of Christianity by simply producing the dead body of Jesus. The simple truth is that they couldn't find His body, they couldn't explain His appearances and they couldn't stop His church.

Other 'explanations' of the resurrection fail to explain it away: the notion that Jesus didn't actually die on the cross (as if the Roman authorities would make such an elementary mistake), that the disciples had hallucinations (as if hundreds of people on different occasions could have the same hallucination) or that the accounts of witnesses were fabrications (as if in those days one would choose women to be the first witnesses in such a scenario). In actual fact, many of the believers were prepared to undergo martyrdom in the name of this risen Lord – something which would be inexplicable on the assumption that they had made up the story.

The continuing existence of the Lord's people (the church), the Lord's book (for Matthew, Mark and the others would never have written their Gospels if they didn't believe in the living Lord) and the Lord's Day (for it would have taken something very significant for Jewish believers to observe Sunday, not the Jewish Saturday Sabbath, as their special day) – these things all point to the factuality of this event which atheism has been unable to explain on its own assumptions.

7. I am not an atheist because of personal and pastoral experience

My final line of approach to the issue – why I am not an atheist – concerns personal and pastoral experience. Forty years' experience

---

13   e.g. John Wenham, *Easter Enigma* (Paternoster, 1984).

as a pastor has confirmed my belief that Christianity 'works'. Through this message of Christ, people have found a liberating sense of forgiveness, an energizing sense of the Holy Spirit's power in their lives and a joyful hope for the future. It won't do for atheism to rubbish such claims.

The experience of Michael Green is typical (though not all can articulate their experience so clearly):

> I was a happy teenager, content with my home, my academic success, my sporting prowess and my friendships, and I stumbled across the greatest friendship of all: that with Jesus Christ. He is the treasure that I have come to value above all else. I was not an emotional cripple looking for a crutch. I was not a romantic looking for a cause. I was not at the bottom of the pile hoping for a leg-up. I was not looking for anything in particular in fact. But I found treasure. That treasure has utterly transformed my life, my goals, my lifestyle.[14]

This is the testimony that I and many others would give, including people I have seen finding the same treasure in the gospel of Jesus Christ. This is not to claim that pastoral experience has always been of Christian 'success', but it is to emphasize the real difference one has seen in the lives of so many who have trusted in Christ.

Michael Green refers to the suspicion that 'religion' appeals especially to emotional cripples, romantics and ne'er-do-wells. As a pastor, my eyebrows are seriously raised when I read the concluding words of a quotation from Dorothy L. Sayers. Writing about Christ's crucifixion, she says:

> The people who hanged Christ never, to do them justice, accused him of being a bore – on the contrary, they thought him too dynamic to be safe. It has been left for later generations to muffle up that shattering personality and surround him with an atmosphere of tedium. We have very efficiently pared the claws of the Lion of Judah, certified him 'meek and mild', and recommended him as a fitting household pet for pale curates and pious old ladies![15]

---

14   Michael Green, *Compelled by Joy* (IVP, 2011), p. 13.

15   From *The Greatest Drama Ever Staged*, quoted in Scripture Union's *Encounter With God*, 31 March 2012.

Pastoral work involves pointing people towards faith in Jesus Christ – not in some ethereal or unworldly way but in relation to the real-life, sometimes harsh, experiences that people encounter day by day. It may be the experience of terminal illness or bereavement, whether the tragic death of children or young people or suicides or sudden loss; it may involve encountering people with alcohol or drug addiction problems (I have never had an actual fisticuffs with anyone, but once had to exit a house quickly before that outcome arose); it obviously concerns marital issues – preparing people for marriage and seeking to help in times of difficulty.

Pastoral experience of meeting with people through all manner of ups and downs of life convinces me that Christianity 'works' and that atheism is a broken cistern that holds no water (Jer. 2:13). I recall the experience of so many who have testified to a peace that passed all human understanding (Phil. 4:7), such as the middle-aged parishioner who lost his health and marriage through multiple sclerosis and yet radiated a peace that was a blessing to all who met him. I think of my wife's testimony of triumphing faith after the stillbirth of our baby son, when she knew the truth of the text: 'Underneath are the everlasting arms.' (Deut. 33:27) I think of a missionary friend in Malawi referring constantly to the way in which she found God's Word through the apostle Paul to be true: 'My grace is sufficient for you.' (2 Cor. 12:9) Other examples could be given, including my own testimony, for all my inadequacies, to the strengthening and guiding hand of the living God.

In this chapter I have given various reasons why I am not an atheist:

- atheism flies in the face of almost universal experience

- the beauty and design of creation implies that there is a Creator

- atheism is often wishful thinking

- the fruits of atheism

- the inadequacy of atheism

- the person and influence of Jesus Christ

- experience that confirms Christ's reality and power

It is not simply a matter of *not* being an atheist. It is much more positive than that. My faith is not based simply on the unviability of atheism but on the truth of Christianity and the reality of Jesus Christ as my Saviour, Lord and Friend.

8

A DEBATER
explains why he is not an Atheist

DAVID ROBERTSON

I spend a great deal of my time debating, discussing with and meeting atheists and agnostics. For the purposes of this essay, I am regarding them as similar; although agnostics are people who say they do not know and indeed cannot know God, to all intents and purposes they live as if there were no God – they are functional atheists. However, an increasing number of people are beginning to self-identify as out-and-out atheists – 14 per cent in the United States and 22 per cent in the United Kingdom. And they are becoming more vocal and militant.

There were times in the past when I wanted to join their ranks. In many ways, atheism was the most attractive option. If there is no God then I don't have to worry about Him, and if there is no life after death then I don't have to worry about that – let us eat, drink and be merry for tomorrow we die.

It was Bertrand Russell who identified these two questions – the existence of God and immortality – as the two key questions. Few people today would know anything about Russell and even fewer would have read his book, *Why I Am Not a Christian and Other Essays*. And yet, although few will have read the book, most will know the arguments, because it is these arguments that are repeated *ad nauseam* on websites, in debates, in the broadcast media and in pubs and cafes throughout the land. In fact, it is Russell's book that provides a starting point for this collection of essays.

It was on 6 March 1927 that he delivered a lecture to the South London Branch of the National Secular Society at Battersea Town Hall. Russell was a member of the British aristocracy who became one of the world's most prominent philosophers and is considered to be one of the founders of analytic philosophy. I personally find his background fascinating and helpful in understanding some of his prejudices and preconceptions.

His father was an atheist who consented to his mother having an affair with his tutor. His mother died when Bertrand was just two years old. When he was four, his father died after a long period of depression, and Russell was brought up by his grandmother, Countess Russell, the wife of the former Prime Minister John Russell.

Bertrand's father had stipulated in the will that he should be brought up as an agnostic – something which the Countess, who was a deeply devoted Scottish Presbyterian, overturned in court. As a result, Bertrand was brought up in a home where prayer and Bible reading were normal. Indeed, he cites his grandmother's favourite verse in *Why I Am Not A Christian* as his motto: 'Thou shalt not follow a multitude to do evil' (Exod. 23:2, KJV).

The young Russell, lonely and suicidal, was fascinated by mathematics and religion. Aged fifteen, he decided there was no such thing as free will; aged seventeen, he decided there was no such thing as life after death, and a year later, he decided that there was no God. He went on to study mathematics at Trinity College, Cambridge, became a lecturer and had a glittering career in philosophy for the rest of this life.

He was an extremely influential character, noted for his pacifism, anti-nuclear bomb stance and his atheism/agnosticism. As regards the latter, his views have largely become the default philosophy of the British elite and those who advocate a secular humanist viewpoint. His private life was very confused; he married four times and had numerous affairs. He died in 1970 at the grand old age of 98.

Apart from his *History of Western Philosophy,* his most famous and influential work is the lecture given in 1927. It was subsequently published in pamphlet form and then became part of a collection of essays, *Why I Am Not a Christian and Other Essays,* a book which has frequently been cited as one of the most influential of the twentieth century. I read this book a number of years ago and only recently returned to it. In this essay, I want to explain why Russell actually drives me towards Christianity rather than away from it. Paradoxically, the very reasons that Russell gives are the reasons that I cannot be an atheist.

It should also be noted how dated and yet how relevant Russell's essay is. It is dated because its science, history and social analyses are so out of date. And yet it is relevant because Russell espouses arguments that are used on the Internet, in newspaper columns and in debates, as though they were somehow shocking new revelations, another advance in the inevitable progress of mankind. Little do many of our progressives realize that all they are espousing are the tired and dated arguments of Bertrand Russell. When I read Richard Dawkins's *The God Delusion,* I realized how the main arguments were just a rehash of Russell's *Why I am Not a Christian,* and so I went back to read it again.

Because Art Requires an Artist I am Not an Atheist

Russell has as the cornerstone of his atheism the question, 'Who created God?' – which he believed killed off the First Cause argument. It still amazes me that an intellectual regards this as a killer point.

The First Cause argument is simply that everything in this world has a cause until you get back to the First Cause, which we call God.

Russell says that that used to make sense to him until at the age of 18 he read John Stuart Mill's autobiography and came to the conclusion that if everything must have a cause then God must have a cause. If there is anything without a cause, then it might as well be the world. In what would now be seen as an incredibly out-of-date and unscientific statement, Russell goes on to argue: 'There is no reason why the world could not have come into being without a cause; nor, on the other hand, is there any reason why it should not have always existed. There is no reason to suppose that the world had a beginning at all.'[1]

Unfortunately for Russell and his followers, we now do have every reason to believe the world did have a beginning. Christians listen to the Bible which tells us: 'In the beginning God created the heavens and the earth.' (Gen. 1:1) Those who do not listen to God speaking in Scripture can then listen to Him speaking in nature. Since the 1950s, science has told us through the Big Bang theory that the universe did indeed have a beginning. Arno Penzias, the Nobel Prize-winning scientist who discovered the background radiation that provided evidence for the Big Bang, declared: 'The best data we have are exactly what I would have predicted, had I nothing to go on but the five books of Moses, the Psalms, the Bible as a whole.'[2] We now know scientifically what the Bible has declared all along.

When John Lennox pointed this out to Richard Dawkins, he rather sniffily responded, 'Well it had a 50:50 chance.' Of course, it did. In fact, there are only two options. To quote Professor Lennox: 'Either human intelligence owes its origin to mindless matter or there is a Creator. It is strange that some people claim that it is their intelligence that leads them to prefer the first to the second.'[3] Indeed.

So I believe in God because it is reasonable, rational and scientific to believe that the creation had a Creator. It did not self-create.

That still leaves the alleged killer problem for Russell, Dawkins and many fourth-form school pupils, 'Who created God?' The

1   All quotes from Russell are from *Why I am Not a Christian and Other Essays on Religion and Related Subjects* (Routledge Classics, 2004).

2   Malcolm Browne, 'Clues to the Universe's Origin Expected' (*New York Times,* 12 March 1978), p. 1.

3   John Lennox, *God's Undertaker* (Lion, 2007), p. 179.

answer is – nobody. None of the monotheistic religions argue for a created God – that is what we call an idol. The point is that God is uncreated. We can either believe in eternal 'stuff' or an eternal Creator. I find the latter to be far more logical and reasonable.

When as a young boy I tried to be an atheist, it was impossible – not because of religious upbringing (indeed, like Russell, I think that would have made it easier) but rather because whenever I walked outside my home, along the Nigg cliffs in Easter Ross in the Scottish Highlands, I found it impossible to believe that all this beauty, creativity and glorious nature was the product of an unguided non-intelligent process. To believe in that would have required a leap of faith greater than any I was being asked to take as a potential Christian.

Another way of putting this argument is that recently revived by the Christian philosopher William Lane Craig – the Kalam cosmological argument. Put simply it states:

- everything that has a beginning of its existence has a cause of its existence

- the universe has a beginning of its existence

- therefore the universe has a cause of its existence

The logic is irrefutable. The evidence is overwhelming. Russell was wrong, although we have to grant that he was living in a much more backward scientific culture and he did not have the knowledge we now have – knowledge that Sir Fred Hoyle once declared shook his atheism more than anything. This is a knowledge which some scientists, after Russell, were reluctant to accept, purely and simply because it destroyed the major premise of the foundational text of their atheism.

This evidence now leads us on to the second argument.

Because There is an Ordered Universe I am Not an Atheist

On the basis of his dismissal of the First Cause argument, Russell then somewhat cavalierly dismissed the natural law and design arguments. Rather than the 'laws' of the universe being given by God, they just simply happen to be. Rather than the world giving evidence of design, it gives evidence of somewhat bad design. 'Do you think that, if you were granted omnipotence and omniscience and millions of years in which to perfect your world, you could produce nothing better than the Ku Klux Klan or the Fascists?'

But Russell again inadvertently highlights two great reasons not to be an atheist.

Firstly, we now know that the argument from design is far deeper and more profound than we ever could have imagined. The fine-tuning of the universe is one of the discoveries of science post-Russell, which greatly undermines his cause. There are fifteen constants in the universe, (gravity, properties of carbon, thermodynamics, etc.), which have to be exactly in tune with one another in order for the universe even to exist. The chances of this happening are so infinitesimal that the odds are a number that is ten to the power of more zeros than atoms that exist in the whole universe!

I heard it put another way: if you took a penny and put it on the ground in the state of Texas, and then covered the whole state of Texas with pennies, and then built them up in a column all the way to the moon, and then did that for the whole US (including Alaska) and then did that 1,000 times, and then you took one of those coins and put a pink dot on it, and randomly inserted it into the pile of coins going all the way to the moon; and then you asked a blindfolded child to pick out the one coin, the chances of the child doing so would be equivalent to the chances of the universe existing with just exactly the right constants all in place. Bertrand Russell was a mathematician but it was not his mathematics that stopped him believing in God.

BECAUSE I AM FEARFULLY AND WONDERFULLY MADE, I AM NOT AN ATHEIST

Another superb mathematician, my friend John Lennox, has been a great help to me in understanding this. He gives another reason to believe – human DNA and the human genome project (the head of which, Francis Collins, is also a Christian).

John Lennox explains it this way. Imagine you go to the beach and as you are walking along you see the words 'I Love You' spelled out in the sand. You naturally assume that there is intelligence behind those words. Someone wrote them. That is the obvious and correct assumption. It is an axiom of science that information does not self-generate. Someone/something has put it there.

Lennox points out that our human bodies are full of a code that would stretch over many thousands of miles, consists only of four letters and yet is essential and unique to every one of us. Why then do you not understand and accept that someone put that code there?

And again the Bible was there before us – 'In the beginning was the Word, and the Word was with God and the Word was God.' (John 1:1) The Logos spoke and the world came into being. The idea of God 'speaking' and things coming into existence is far more plausible now that we understand that everything consists of information!

Robert Jastrow, in his book *God and the Astronomers,* writes: 'For the scientist who has lived by his faith in the power of reason, the story ends like a bad dream. He has scaled the mountain of ignorance; he is about to conquer the highest peak; as he pulls himself over the final rock, he is greeted by a band of theologians who have been sitting there for centuries.'[4]

The more I get to know about the human body, the more I am amazed by it. In the latter part of 2011 I spent several weeks in hospital seriously ill. Through the skill of the medical staff and, I believe, the intervention of God in answer to the prayers of His people, I recovered. One of the legacies of that experience has been to leave me with a heightened sense of wonder at the marvels of creation, including my own battered and weary body. God is the great designer.

BECAUSE THERE IS EVIL I AM NOT AN ATHEIST

Russell does not understand why there is evil in the world. Like so many before and after, he basically declares: if I were God I would have done a better job.

Now let us assume there is no God. What difference would that make? There would still be suffering, evil, death and sorrow.

---

4   Robert Jastrow, *God and the Astronomers* (W.W. Norton, 2000).

Removing God does not solve the problem. There would still be the KKK and the Fascists, or Al Qaeda, or the Communists, or the child slave traders, or the millions of paedophiles ...

This great problem of evil was what drove me to Christ. At university I studied Weimar and Nazi Germany; the big question for me was why human beings could behave in such a way. Germany was not, after all, a backward nation of primitive savages, but rather the most advanced, cultured, scientific, progressive nation in the world, and yet it was a nation that gave rise to the Holocaust.

The fact that such a thing could happen blows away Russell's optimism that human beings would just continue to progress as science advanced. The problem of evil makes no sense unless you recognize categories of good and evil, and it is difficult to do so without some absolute standard – and that is difficult without an absolute Lawgiver.

That still leaves the problem of why God would allow suffering or create a world in which suffering was even possible. Russell's simplistic, literalist analysis that God is responsible for creating Fascism only works if you assume that God is responsible for everything and that there is no possibility of free will or indeed human responsibility.

Russell came to the position first of all that there was no free will, and then to the position that there was no God. The tragedy, of course, is that it does not end there. In taking away both free will and God, you end up in the position where you ultimately deny the essence of humanity.

BECAUSE THERE IS MORALITY I AM NOT AN ATHEIST

And you also deny the fact of morality. After the Second World War, Russell was being interviewed on the BBC Home Service and came out with the statement that 'Dachau (the Nazi concentration camp) is wrong' is not a fact. I quoted this during a debate at the University of Cambridge and my opponent challenged me to prove that Dachau was wrong. He said he felt it was wrong but he could not prove it was wrong as a fact in the same way that gravity is a fact.

My response? We were at different starting points. He started with the view that there was no God and because of that he ended up in the unenviable position of not being able to prove that the Holocaust was wrong. I started with the view that the Holocaust was wrong and when I asked why, and kept asking, I ended up with God, and so I could say it was wrong. The argument from morality is not that Christians are more moral; it is that without God an absolute morality is almost impossible, as morality only becomes a social construct. With God, there is good. Without God, there is chaos.

If I had the power, I could easily create a world in which you did not suffer, experience sorrow or have broken relationships. I could make you into a chair. You would experience no pain, no sorrow, no hatred. But then you would experience no pleasure, no joy and no love. You would live in this blissfully unaware state. That may be Buddhist nirvana but it is not human.

But if I were to create a world in which you had the freedom to choose good and evil, to love or hate, to rejoice and to think, then I am absolutely certain that I could not have done better than God. Perhaps the price of human freedom and love is the KKK and Fascism?

An atheist has no answer to the problem of evil and suffering, other than *suck it up and see*. A Christian does – Christ. This brings me on to another great reason for not being an atheist.

BECAUSE OF JESUS CHRIST I AM NOT AN ATHEIST
Russell did not like Jesus Christ. He had a somewhat simplistic, caricatured version of His teaching (for example, he argues that no Christian should be a judge because Jesus said, 'Do not judge'!), expressed doubts as to whether He existed at all and condemned Him for believing in hell.

Again, it is a simplistic and rather twisted understanding of the teaching of Christ, alleging, for example, that Jesus criticized the Pharisees because they did not like His preaching, when the reality was that He condemned them because they were hypocrites using religion to oppress the people. But when I read the teaching of Jesus Christ, when I see His miracles and His acts of compassion, when I observe His radicalism and His kindness, I cannot but be drawn to Him.

I am reminded of the teaching in Hebrews:

> In the past God spoke to our ancestors through the prophets at many times and in various ways, but in these last days he has spoken to us by his Son, whom he appointed heir of all things, and through whom he also made the universe. The Son is the radiance of God's glory and the exact representation of his being, sustaining all things by his powerful word. (Heb. 1:1-3a)

If I want to know what God is like, then I look at Christ.

Logic, reason and science tell me that there is a Creator; they tell me of His divine nature and eternal power (Rom. 1:18) but they do not tell me of a Saviour. They do not tell me of the God of love, justice and mercy. Christ does.

Furthermore ,when I see what Christ did for me – 'The Son of God loved me and gave himself for me.' (Gal. 2:20) – then I am stunned and amazed. 'This is love: not that we loved God, but that he loved us, and gave his Son as the atoning sacrifice for our sins.' (1 John 4:10)

BECAUSE OF THE CHURCH I AM NOT AN ATHEIST

This is surprising for many people. It has become fashionable, even amongst professing Christians, for people to declare that they love Jesus but don't like the church. Indeed the church is probably a major reason why many people do not believe – at least at a superficial and emotional level.

Russell hated the church with a passion:

> You find as you look around the world that every single bit of progress in humane feeling, every improvement in the criminal law, every step toward the diminution of war, every step toward better treatment of the coloured races, or every mitigation of slavery, every moral progress that there has been in the world, has been consistently opposed by the organized churches of the world. I say quite deliberately that the Christian religion, as organized in its churches, has been and still is the principal enemy of moral progress in the world.

It is all high-flown rhetoric and largely unhistorical, hysterical nonsense, but it has had its desired effect. Just as in Weimar Germany, some politicians and social theorists looked for someone to blame ('it's all the fault of the Jews'), so in today's Western world there are people who really do believe that the church is the primary source of evil within the world.

Steven Weinberg rather chillingly declares: 'With or without religion, you would have good people doing good things and evil people doing evil things. But for good people to do evil things, that takes religion.'[5] The New Atheists take up on Russell's hatred of the church and turn it into an attack on religion as a virus. And what should happen with a virus? It should be eradicated.

Such hatred only comes from ignorance and prejudice. Just as it was very difficult for any Germans who had normal dealings with Jews to regard them as vermin, so it is very difficult for anyone who comes across the church of Jesus Christ to write it off as a source of all evil. I was strongly opposed to Christianity and the church but it was the love and actions of Christians that helped persuade me there was a great deal more to it than I thought.

Today it is still the case that the best 'apologia' for the gospel is the church of Jesus Christ where Christ's command to love is obeyed and His prophecy about effective witness is fulfilled. 'By this all people will know that you are my disciples, if you have love for one another.' (John 13:35, ESV)

Of course, I am fully aware that the church often does things wrong and that there are people in the church who disgrace the name of Christ, but then the Bible explains this by pointing out that we are all sinners and we have to battle against the evil within all our lives. What amazes me is that in the midst of such ugliness I can still find the beautiful bride of Christ. The Christian view is both realistic (recognizing the ugliness) and restorative (seeing the beauty). This leads us on to another reason for not being an atheist.

---

5   Steven Weinberg, *New York Times*, 20 April 1999.

BECAUSE I AM NOT A UTOPIAN I AM NOT AN ATHEIST

Bertrand Russell had an incredible faith. He believed in progress. He believed, like Weinberg, that for good men to do evil it required religion. He believed that the world 'needs hope for the future, not looking back all the time toward a past that is dead, which we trust will be far surpassed by the future that our intelligence can create.'

He believed that science could recreate man:

> When we have discovered how character depends upon physiological conditions, we shall be able, if we choose, to produce far more of the type of human being that we admire. Intelligence, artistic capacity, benevolence – all these things no doubt could be increased by science. There seems scarcely any limit to what could be done in the way of producing a good world, if only men would use science wisely.

His was a utopianism that became dangerous. He opposed the rearmament of Britain against Hitler, although he was strongly against Hitler. He believed in peace and progress – great ideas but not entirely realistic.

The philosopher John Gray, in his wonderful but depressing book, *Black Mass,* points out how secular utopianism was just as dangerous as religious utopianism. He cites Lewis Namier: 'Hitler and the Third Reich were the gruesome and incongruous consummation of an age, which, as none other, believed in progress and felt assured it was being achieved.'[6]

I am not an atheist because I do not share Russell's faith in the inevitable progress of humanity. He was speaking from the context of a particular culture – one in which he was part of the elite, where he had been taught about his own class and race superiority, and who believed that he had the answers.

In fact, his belief in progress and morality was greatly undermined by his own actions – by their fruit you shall know them. His commitments in marriage largely depended on how he felt and what

---

6   John Gray, *Black Mass: Apocalyptic Religion and the Death of Utopia* (Allen Lane, 2007), p. 55.

he was looking for. His teachings on sex and marriage seemed to be more about justifying his own sexual immorality than about any concepts of truth, good or beauty. In one infamous passage, he even went so far as to argue that women teachers should not be virgins!

> ... everybody who has taken the trouble to study morbid psychology knows that prolonged virginity is, as a rule, extraordinarily harmful to women, so harmful that, in a sane society, it would be severely discouraged in teachers. The restrictions imposed lead more and more to a refusal, on the part of energetic and enterprising women, to enter the teaching profession. This is all due to the lingering influence of superstitious asceticism.

The Muslim heaven may be populated with virgins for the man; Russell's utopia was populated by 'sexually liberated' women, who would, of course, be available for the man too! Well, Russell is getting his 'sexually liberated' Britain in the twenty-first century – although one suspects it has not done much for education.

Because I am Afraid I am not an Atheist

Here I seem to be agreeing with Russell. He declares: 'Religion is based, I think, primarily and mainly upon fear.' In one sense he is right. There are things we are afraid of, and so we should be. Russell was afraid of nuclear war, and rightly so. He was afraid of ignorance and disease – again, rightly so.

I too have many fears. But three of them I do not share with Russell. I am afraid of death because it is the last enemy. I am afraid of myself because I know a little of the corruption of my own heart. And I am afraid of God because He is a being greater than I can conceive of and awesome in His holiness. And that is why I am a Christian – because Christ has killed death, renewed my heart and brought me into the presence of God the Father. He deals with all my fears.

Because I have a sense of Hope and Eternity I am not an Atheist

Although Russell's view of humanity in general and his own group in particular was optimistic in the short term, in the long term his view of the universe was depressingly bleak:

Moreover, if you accept the ordinary laws of science, you have to suppose that human life and life in general on this planet will die out in due course: it is a stage in the decay of the solar system; at a certain stage of decay you get the sort of conditions of temperature and so forth which are suitable to protoplasm, and there is life for a short time in the life of the whole solar system. You see in the moon the sort of thing to which the earth is tending – something dead, cold, and lifeless.

I don't accept that. Long before Russell, the wisest man in the world, King Solomon, reflected on the meaning of life, the universe and everything. He wrote down his struggles in a marvellous book, which, although 3,000 years old, is as relevant today as it ever was. Indeed it has dated a lot less than *Why I Am Not a Christian*.

In Ecclesiastes, Solomon reflects upon the fact that 'under the sun' everything is meaningless. The phrase 'under the sun' is used several times and is the key to understanding the whole book. It simply means 'without God'. If you accept Russell's philosophy then 'dead, cold, and lifeless' is what this world is going to become. It is what you are going to become. That might be more palatable if you are a wealthy member of the English aristocracy with a plentiful supply of wine, women and song – but it does not offer the rest of us much hope, and ultimately is even hopeless for them.

There is an alternative. And it is one that is not wishful thinking, sky fairies or myth.

Ecclesiastes 3:10-11 says: 'I have seen the burden God has laid on men. He has made everything beautiful in its time. He has also set eternity in the hearts of men; yet they cannot fathom what God has done from beginning to end.' That's the key. God has made us with this burden of humankind. We have an awareness of beauty, transcendence and something beyond. But we are in the dark. We cannot see – which is why He sent His Son Jesus Christ to be the light of the world. Logos, Love and Light bring Life.

That is why I am not an atheist.

9

A THEOLOGIAN
explains why he is not an Atheist

CHRIS SINKINSON

The first atheist I ever met was my father. He was interested in spiritual things, and an artist by profession, but he did not believe in a god in any orthodox sense. As a child, that gave me plenty of opportunities to debate matters of faith. Did my father have anything against God or any strong argument against His existence? I never heard any such reasons. However, he did have a strong dislike of what he called organized religion. As a young man during the Second World War, he refused to participate in the military and this coloured his view of religion as a force that blindly compelled people to do terrible things. Like Bertrand Russell, my father was a pacifist.

My dad encouraged me to think for myself and I have come to believe that he was right in some ways. We should not trust authorities and institutions blindly. We should question ideas and test beliefs. Through that process, I have become persuaded that God exists and that there are sound philosophical and historical reasons to believe in Him.

DIGGING IN THE DIRT

I had always wanted to be an archaeologist. My first summer job was working with the Test Valley Archaeological Trust and, from there,

I went to Southampton University to study archaeology. Through this experience, I realized that I had made a mistake. Having spent too many afternoons standing around in rain-soaked English fields, I realized that archaeology was not for me. It was not just the rain. My real interest was in people, and why they thought the way they did. I transferred from archaeology to philosophy at university in order to pursue these themes – and to avoid having to spend Saturdays in the rain.

It was while in my late teens that I became a Christian. Like many converts, my experience was not a single moment but a progressive change of heart and mind. The first key experience was found in the example of students who were members of a college lunchtime Christian Union. They debated things. They talked and prayed. They knew God as a personal friend. They were decent people. This was not the lure of organized religion or club membership. This was the example of real people with real faith living real lives. And I wanted that too. I came to faith in Christ through their witness to me.

My interests in archaeology and philosophy only served to strengthen and deepen what I had come to believe. It was not as if I didn't meet plenty of atheists. Many of the philosophy lecturers, students and authors I encountered provided me with examples of atheism as a live option. But it was the Christian lecturers (there were two I knew in the Philosophy department), students and authors who provided the more appealing alternative.

I am not an atheist because that world view does not satisfy the evidences of experience, history and reason. I have been persuaded more and more of the truth of that famous remark by Francis Bacon:

> It is true that a little philosophy inclines man's mind to atheism; but depth in philosophy brings man's mind to religion.[1]

PHILOSOPHY DID NOT ENCOURAGE ATHEISM

I had one significant problem with philosophy. I enjoyed reading but most philosophical texts were difficult to read and many were inelegant as literature! However, a few philosophers stood out

---

1   A number of important Christian philosophers explain the reasons for their faith in Kelly James Clark (ed.), *Philosophers Who Believe* (Downers Grove, IL: IVP, 1993).

as good reading. One such was Bertrand Russell. His *History of Western Philosophy* appeared on not a single course reading list but was a useful crib sheet for understanding at least Russell's opinion on the intellectual giants of the past. That led me to read the entertaining collection of his essays published together as *Why I am Not a Christian.*

Bertrand Russell stated very clearly his own reasons for rejecting any form of supernatural religion. His intellectual objection to religion is the familiar one repeated by the New Atheists of our own time. Materialism is able to account for all our observations and experiences. There is no need for a religious explanation. What is the human being? In an essay first published in 1925, Russell wrote: 'We are part of nature, we are subordinated to nature, the outcome of natural laws, and their victims in the long run.'[2] If we are nothing more than material objects in a closed universe of cause and effect, then there is no need to appeal to God, the soul, heaven or hell. There is no purpose, objective moral order or transcendent significance to anything. The same commitment to materialism is maintained today by the 'New' Atheists: 'The universe we observe has precisely the properties we should expect if there is, at bottom, no design, no purpose, no evil and no good, nothing but blind, pitiless indifference.'[3]

Materialism as a world view has never satisfied me, even as a possible option. Of course, not all atheists need to be materialists. Zen Buddhism is atheistic but not materialist.[4] However, in my experience, most Western atheists hold to a materialist view. Famously, C. S. Lewis presented a case against such materialism in his *Mere Christianity*. I read this as an undergraduate. Having enjoyed the Narnia chronicles, I wanted to read what Lewis had to say about philosophical matters.

---

2   Bertrand Russell, *A History of Western Philosophy*, p. 47.

3   Richard Dawkins, *River out of Eden* (London: Weidenfeld & Nicolson), p. 133.

4   Paul Williams, formerly Director of Buddhist Studies at the University of Bristol, affirms that this is true not only of Zen; 'Buddhists do not believe in the existence of God.' There is no place for the existence of a God conceived along any traditional lines. *The Unexpected Way* (Edinburgh: T&T Clark, 2002), p. 25.

Lewis starts his case with the moral judgments that we all casually make during the course of any day. When we describe something as good, bad or unfair, we are appealing to some kind of objective standard. So what about the moral debates and disagreements people have? Do those moral disagreements not undermine the idea of an objective moral order?

Lewis had a number of important responses. He pointed out that, even when we dispute a particular moral teaching, we are still appealing to an objective standard. How else can we have a moral dilemma? 'The moment you say that one set of moral ideas can be better than another, you are, in fact, measuring them both by a standard ... the standard that measures two things is something different from either.'[5] Lewis built a careful case that the very possibility of moral debate is a signpost towards supernatural reality. This point does not, in itself, prove the existence of God. But it does expose the weakness of materialism. If we concede that there is at least one non-material thing which objectively exists, then materialism is simply not enough.

Can an atheist reply to C. S. Lewis's argument? Of course! You will hear critics dismiss Lewis as offering *non sequiturs*, 'straw man' arguments or building a house of cards. But no one can lightly dismiss Lewis as a fool. He was a great scholar, a capable debater and trained in classical logic. So is the moral argument outlined by Lewis just bewitching bluster or does he make a cogent case?

One reason for lofty dismissals of Lewis's argument rests on a misunderstanding of what *Mere Christianity* is seeking to do. Lewis is offering an inference to the best explanation. He appeals to our ordinary experience as a signpost to a transcendent reality. The analogies employed by Lewis are carefully chosen to help persuade us that the inference is sensible. Alister McGrath explains: 'Lewis' approach ... does not have the logical force of a deductive proof. It is much better understood as a further demonstration of the intrinsic reasonableness of the Christian faith.'[6] Christianity accounts for our intuitive sense that there is an objective moral order.

---

5   C. S. Lewis *Mere Christianity* (London: Collins), p. 23.

6   Alister McGrath, *Mere Apologetics* (Grand Rapids: Baker Books, 2012), p. 107. Of course, the moral argument can be presented in a more robust deductive form. See William Lane Craig, *On Guard* (Colorado Springs: David C. Cook, 2010), pp. 127-45.

Morality is not just a description of what people do in any given circumstance. Morality is not another word for desire, emotion or taste. Morality is a non-material reality and its existence refutes materialism. It is misleading to imply that Lewis was proving the existence of God from our moral sense. Lewis himself concludes his case for objective morality by stating we are 'not yet within a hundred miles of the God of Christian morality.'[7] What we may infer is the existence of a non-material order of reality. Not all real things are physical objects composed of atoms. There is a chink in the armour of materialism. The door is left open a crack. What may seem like a small point is of enormous significance. Like a door left just slightly ajar, the light that streams through from outside is enough to fill a room.[8]

What I found helpful in reading C. S. Lewis is that he kept broadening horizons and not shrinking them. Many of his arguments follow a similar pattern of moving from a common human experience, whether grief or joy, towards a transcendent reality that explains our experiences.

THE INADEQUACY OF MATERIALISM

In contrast, I found the materialistic philosophy untrue, unworkable and uninspiring. Bertrand Russell asserted, 'Superstition is the origin of moral rules.'[9] If that is true, then presumably moral rules are a bad idea. Moral rules should be relegated to the dustbin of history along with other outdated superstitions. Russell had his own explanation of morality: 'It is we who create value and our desires which confer value. In this realm we are kings, and we debase our kingship if we bow down to Nature. It is for us to determine the good life, not for Nature – not even for Nature personified as God.'[10]

---

7   op. cit., p. 33.

8   It is hard to overestimate the enormous impact of C. S. Lewis's short book. Francis Collins, head of the Human Genome Project and one of the world's leading scientists, identifies it as a key in his own conversion from atheism to Christianity. See Francis Collins, *The Language of God* (London: Simon & Schuster, 2007), pp. 21-31.

9   Bertrand Russell, *Why I am Not a Christian*, p. 54.

10   ibid., p. 49.

This definition of value helps explain Russell's own moral vacillations. In the immediate post-war period, he campaigned for America to make pre-emptive nuclear war against the menace of Stalinist Russia, while a decade later he was denouncing America as evil for failing to unilaterally disarm.[11] Everyone is entitled to change their minds and admit they were wrong, but by what standard do we do so? And Russell's embarrassing attempt to deny he had ever made his earlier claims is all the more unsettling. What is the moral standard by which our views may be judged better or worse? In a 1961 speech, Russell declared: 'We used to think Hitler was wicked when he wanted to kill all the Jews. But Kennedy and Macmillan not only want to kill all the Jews but all the rest of us too.' By what standard was he able to take his muddled evidence and say of the British Prime Minister and American President, 'They are much more wicked than Hitler'?[12]

Materialism is ultimately self-refuting. It tries to speak of things for which it has no vocabulary. This problem raises its head when a materialist describes morality, values, goodness and even when they try to deal with evil.

The problem of evil and suffering is particularly interesting here. As an objection to the existence of God, it initially seems to command great weight. How could a good, all-powerful God allow evil in the world? But as an objection it does rely on our ability to state what evil is. If evil is measured by an objective moral standard and describes those things to which God is opposed ,then we certainly have the difficult question to pose: why does God allow such things? But if there is no objective measure, if evil describes only things we do not like, if suffering is simply part of material processes then there is no problem to solve. There is no evil to confront, no ultimate purpose in doing good, no greater vision of life that should command our attention. I would prefer to have the problem of evil than for evil to not be a problem.

---

11 The moral character of Russell on this and other issues is explored by Paul Johnson in *Intellectuals* (New York: Harper, 1988), pp. 197-224.

12 Cited in Paul Johnson, ibid., p. 209.

The Source of Morality

The dead ends of materialistic philosophy are all around us. For example, Richard Dawkins tries to explain moral behaviour in terms compatible with materialism. He attributes altruism to a by-product of evolutionary processes. There is no ultimate meaning to pity other than it being a misfiring of our sexual desires. 'We can no more help ourselves feeling pity when we see a weeping unfortunate (who is unrelated and unable to reciprocate) than we can help ourselves feeling lust for a member of the opposite sex (who may be infertile or otherwise unable to reproduce). Both are misfirings, Darwinian mistakes: blessed, precious mistakes.'[13]

Richard Dawkins describes evolutionary processes that could explain why we behave the way we do. But he has done nothing to explain morality. The real question is not 'why' we do something but why we 'should' do something. If only Dawkins had read Lewis a little more carefully he might have presented a better case. Lewis wrote: 'Electrons and molecules behave in a certain way, and certain results follow, and that may be the whole story. But men behave in a certain way and that is not the whole story, for all the time you know that they ought to behave differently.'[14] Dawkins knows that this is the case because he slips in the word 'blessed' and 'precious' to describe those evolutionary mistakes. He cannot resist moving from factual description to moral evaluation because materialism is not enough. It is too limited a philosophical world view to account for reality. Atheists end up in the self-refuting position of trying to deny something they must affirm. They want to deny objective morality – and think it objectively good to do so.

The existence of a moral law is one of many clues to transcendent reality. It is part of our general intuition that we are not mere collections of physical components in a closed universe of cause and effect. Atheists try to explain moral behaviour in purely material terms but, time and again, they find themselves explaining something else. They may describe what creatures do in any given

13   Richard Dawkins, *The God Delusion* (London: Bantam, 2006), p. 221.

14   *Mere Christianity*, pp. 26-7.

circumstance or why their genetic make-up compels them to behave in a certain way. All such explanations miss the point. They fail to explain *why* we ought to behave in a certain way. Like clever street magicians, materialists can distract us with powerful evolutionary accounts of our behaviour, while sneaking unwarranted moral judgments into their performance.

The philosophers I found most helpful to read were those who had a more expansive view of reality. That led me to pursue doctoral study on the relationship of Christianity to other religions and the work of the British philosopher of religion John Hick. One of Hick's most influential projects has been to develop a new way of understanding the compatibility of religions. While I disagreed fundamentally with Hick's approach to the world religions, I found him a philosopher who took seriously the signposts to transcendence all around us.[15]

The very existence of the world religions makes this evident. Theism has greater explanatory power than the alternatives. Sometimes the plurality of world religions is taken as evidence against Christianity. This never made sense to me. If there is a God then one would expect some kind of knowledge of God's existence to be natural and common the world over. Furthermore, one would expect there to be confused accounts, erroneous ideas and some deliberate distortions. To believe that Jesus Christ is the only Saviour does not entail that I deny other religions have any true insights into supernatural reality. In fact, on the contrary, I would expect there to be a general awareness of the existence of God. But the materialist has to deny that any religion is valid.

However, the critics of the moral argument, whether in the form given at a popular level by C. S. Lewis or in a more complex, philosophical form by Immanuel Kant, seem to delight in the reply that morality alone cannot prove the existence of the God of Christianity. Such a reply misses the point. The moral argument is an inference from universally available evidence. We make inferences from appropriate evidence all the time. Discovering the

---

15   Chris Sinkinson, *The Universe of Faiths* (Carlisle: Paternoster, 2000).

ruined foundations of a great city in a desert landscape would entitle us to infer the existence of a historical city with real inhabitants at a real point in time. The fact that critics might infer something different or attempt to attribute its existence to the random effects of weathering would not undermine the claim that the best inference is to the existence of historical inhabitants in times past who built these ancient dwellings. Likewise, the existence of a moral law is evidence from which we are entitled to infer the existence of a moral lawgiver.

So why don't all philosophers agree? Why are some convinced by the moral argument for God's existence and others consider it of no merit? The study of philosophy confirms that there is no such thing as neutral knowledge. The evidence is interpreted according to presuppositions and assumptions. What counts as a 'best' inference will depend on many hidden factors. This has been confirmed to me time and again in my study of the Bible.

BACK TO EARTH

My own interest in archaeology has been reawakened through teaching theology. Opportunities to be part of an excavation in Galilee and teach archaeological background to the Bible have only continued to highlight the role of inference and interpretation in weighing up the value of material evidence.

Does archaeology prove the Bible? I am asked this from time to time. The question misunderstands the role of archaeology. The study of ruins and remains provides data that, for the most part, help us understand the ancient world, including its culture and customs. Only rarely is there direct evidence for a specific event from the ancient world. Even historical figures well known from written sources have left little or no trace in the physical remains gathered by archaeologists. These are not unique issues for the archaeology of the Bible; this is true of archaeology throughout the world.[16]

---

16   For a helpful survey of these issues in archaeology and the challenge of what is called biblical 'minimalism', see Victor H. Matthews, *Studying the Ancient Israelites: A Guide to Sources and Methods* (Nottingham: Apollos, 2007).

ARCHAEOLOGY AND THE BIBLE

So what is the role of archaeology? Rather than proving miracles, it provides the basis for testing and affirming that the records gathered together in the collection we call the Bible are historical records. Wherever they can be tested they demonstrate accurate knowledge of the times about which they speak. Despite the scepticism of some, time after time new discoveries have served to confirm the reliability and trustworthiness of the text.

The place names and customs of Genesis fit with the Middle Bronze Age context in which it is set. People groups once known only through the biblical record, like the Hittites, have subsequently been identified through their extensive material remains. Until recently, it was fashionable to dismiss King David as a character of legend or myth. An absence of evidence was taken as evidence of his absence. Surely, the critics complained, if we only have the biblical record to rely upon, then we have no good grounds to affirm his existence? Kenneth Kitchen brings this particular complaint up to date:

> One minute biblical David did not exist (we were told), because no scrap of firsthand evidence was available to vouch for him. Then, some eighteen months later, the Tel Dan stela most unkindly brushed this silly, asinine myth aside, by evidencing him as (a) real and (b) as a dynastic founder, to which was added 'House of [Da]vid' on the Mesha stele – both only about 140 years after David's time. Then, possibly closer still, a Negev toponym in the great list of Shoshenq I (924) quite likely names a 'heights of David,' less than 50 years after the old fellow's decease, when the memory of him would still be fresh.[17]

Now the fashion regarding King David is to concede his existence but deny he was more than a local chief, with no monumental building work to his name. But current archaeological excavation

---

17   K. A. Kitchen, *On the Reliability of the Old Testament* (Grand Rapids: Eerdmans, 2003), pp. 483-4.

in Jerusalem is uncovering significant remains that are likely to prove to be what is left of the palace of King David.[18]

Archaeology may not prove a miracle has taken place, but it can provide evidence that the text is reliable. And if it is reliable in those areas where it is open to testing then we have good grounds to trust it in areas where it is not open to testing. The extraordinary wealth of remains that illustrate the reliability of the biblical writers in matters that we can test gives us good grounds to trust its eyewitness record of matters that do not leave direct material evidence.[19]

I see no grounds to hold a sceptical view of the contents of the Bible and this leads me to the most foundational reason for not being an atheist. The continuing impact of Jesus of Nazareth on my life and the lives of so many down through history is the most compelling reason for faith. I am persuaded that the historical evidences for the empty tomb of Jesus found in the Bible match a present experience of a living Saviour.

God is not only an abstract inference at the end of a chain of reasoning whether from experience or from history. God is also the starting point from which we can make sense of life. Because I believe in God, I have a basis for objective morality and a faith that is grounded in real historical events.[20]

CONCLUSION

So I am not an atheist for a number of overlapping reasons. But underlying all those reasons is the conviction that Christianity is true.

I agree with my late father that there is much in organized religion that I want no part in. Nor am I particularly interested

---

18   For a recent appraisal of the evidence so far, see Avraham Faust, 'Did Eliat Mazar Find David's Palace?', *Biblical Archaeological Review*, September/October 2012, Vol. 38, No. 5. Faust is not so sure but he concludes that it is quite possible that archaeologist Mazar has indeed found a structure that served as King David's palace.

19   For an enjoyable and readable romp through the evidence see Randall Price, *The Stones Cry Out: What Archaeology Reveals about the Truth of the Bible* (Oregon: Harvest House Publishers, 1997).

20   I expand on a wider range of reasons in Chris Sinkinson, *Confident Christianity* (Nottingham: IVP, 2012).

in rituals and traditions. But my experience of Christians and of church never led me to atheism. I saw good reasons, honest people, and shared in genuine experience of the living God.

I share McGrath's assessment that 'the rise of atheism in the West was undoubtedly a protest against a corrupted and complacent church; yet paradoxically, it has energized Christianity to reform itself, in ways that seriously erode the credibility of those earlier criticisms.'[21] Atheism serves the church as a protest movement – helping Christians to reflect and reform.

But as a serious alternative to faith in Christ I fail to find any appeal. However, I do want to be part of a movement of God's people seeking both a credible explanation of the reasons for their faith *and* living a credible life of integrity and love.

---

21   Alister McGrath, *The Twilight of Atheism: The Rise and Fall of Disbelief in the Modern World* (London: Random House, 2004), p. 277.

10

A JOURNALIST
explains why she is not an Atheist
HEATHER TOMLINSON

Once I was a hard-nosed, hard-drinking, cynical and bolshie young journalist. There were a few things that really got me excited. The thrill of getting a good news story and the camaraderie down the pub were my main source of satisfaction in life. I was a journalist on national newspapers and I loved it. The job is a licence to be nosy, to meet loads of interesting people and to ask difficult questions.

I was highly opinionated, thinking I knew what was true: the church was boring, Christians were hypocritical and bigoted, and the answer to the world's problems was liberal socialism or a watered-down version of it. Doubt did not enter my mind on these points. I had secular, liberal attitudes about sex and relationships, and I partied hard. If someone had told me that in a few years' time I would be a fairly conservative, evangelical Christian, I'd have laughed in their face.

A LOVE FOR SCIENCE
I've always liked difficult questions and getting good answers to them. I was bored at school because things were too easy, but I had good science teachers who sparked an interest in the beauty and

logic of biology and chemistry. I loved science – everything was clear: black or white, yes or no.

It was through the inspiration of these teachers that I ended up doing a university degree in molecular biology. I loved the subject. Exploring the intricate machinery that ticks away in every cell of our bodies evoked a great sense of awe, wonder and fascination for the material world. I wasn't cut out for a life in a laboratory, but I loved to study hard science.

But these were the days before science was being claimed as a reason not to believe in God by the likes of Richard Dawkins. In fact at the end of the degree, I was more sure that there was a God than I was before I started; the complexity inspired too much awe. I didn't think it could have come about solely by chance, although I saw that there was good evidence of some kind of evolutionary process. This did not in any way contradict the reality of a God, however, and I still believe this to be the case, both before and after my conversion – I think that somehow God worked through evolution to create life. My basic belief in God had existed since my childhood, though at times I might have called myself agnostic. I ticked the 'spiritual but not religious' box in surveys, but I did turn to God in prayer at key points of my life.

LIFE AS A JOURNALIST

After five years on national newspapers, I believe that it was prayer that took me out of this environment. I had originally wanted to be a journalist to 'do good' in the world – to expose wrongdoing and champion the cause of the underdog. It was pretty obvious to me that this was not what I was achieving, however much I loved the lifestyle.

I prayed one night, 'God, what should I do?' There was no flash of lightning, but I believe it set in motion a massive change in my life. I joke to my friends that I had to leave newspapers to get saved. I think there may be a grain of truth in it. I was so absorbed in the adrenaline rush of living in London and the Fleet Street culture that I needed to be out of that environment to be able to explore more spiritual paths.

I decided I was going to retrain – as a clinical psychologist, a career I thought would use my interest in people, my love of investigating and my fascination with science all together, as well as making the world a better place. This wasn't an easy change, and clinical psychology is about as competitive as journalism. It involved doing another degree – in Psychology – and doing some hard graft on the deeply distressing acute mental health wards of the National Health Service. But I like a challenge, and I left London and the national press to work in hospitals and go back to studying.

As I worked with people who were in great suffering, I wondered if I had found a new answer to the world's problems: the transformation of the individual through the care and concern of a therapist. My leftist beliefs were that all problems were caused by the environment and upbringing of a person – whether they had been really loved and cared for as a child. The retraining of a damaged person by a psychologist could lead to a modern utopia, I thought – no crime and perfect peace.

There is a little bit of truth to this; psychological therapy can be really helpful for some people. But some of the pain people experienced could not be blamed on others, and was about personal choices. Some people labelled 'mentally ill' were actually the most interesting, lovely and unique human beings, who were often treated terribly. Being face-to-face with some of the worst of the totally undeserved suffering of people in our country, as well as some of the worst behaviour and recklessness, provoked a lot of deep thinking.

SEARCHING

I felt that I needed some kind of spirituality in my life. Although I had loved the jobs I had done, they had never really satisfied me deep within, and the relationships I had been in had never done so, and usually ended up in pain for me, or in my inflicting pain on others. The relationships I observed around me seemed to be similarly unsatisfying.

Although I was looking for something spiritual, I couldn't have articulated what it was. Now I look back and I know that what

I was looking for was love. And I knew I wanted to love others too. But sometimes I found it difficult to always maintain compassion, even when I wanted to. I had also got a bit bored of drinking and living a 'party' lifestyle. I had tried all the experiences that the world had to offer and I wasn't feeling satisfied. So I started reading around.

My first choice would have been Buddhism as it's a bit cooler than most of the 'religions' out there. I attended a few meditation classes and read a few books, but it didn't seem to go deep enough. I remember going out on a date with a Buddhist; he said his aim was to lose all his emotions and attachments to people. This idea didn't appeal, and neither did dating someone who thought like this.

I also read the Koran, parts of the Bible and other kinds of spiritual writings. I felt very angry about organized religion, because I perceived that it oppressed women, promoted violence or discriminated against gay people. I had bought into the world's idea that the worst evils of the world are racism, sexism and homophobia, whereas now I think that it is hatred for any human being that is the problem, not just hatred that is discriminating against a group.

But this desire for equality is the reason that for a short period, I was interested in paganism and Wicca, which is the fashionable term for witchcraft these days. Thankfully I never actually got involved with any spells, or so on. I read books about it, and I liked its reverence for nature, its alleged equality between the genders and its claim to be the original religion of the British Isles. But something bugged me. If it was the authentic religion of the British, why was the reference work (which is called *The Book of Shadows*) written in the last two centuries?

I think that God intervened. I rarely entered our local library, but I did at this time, and 'happened' to glance at an academic book about the paganism of pre-Christian Britain. I read it with interest, as it was answering exactly the question that was bugging me. The book basically told me that we actually know very little about what pagans did, but that there was some evidence of bestiality and human sacrifice. That was the end of my interest in paganism.

DON'T ALL RELIGIONS LEAD TO GOD?

At the time, the idea of a dogmatic and 'exclusive' religion really bothered me. Surely all religions lead to God – why claim that your own is the best? It seemed intolerant and ignorant. But, looking back, my beliefs about pluralism and liberalism were just as intolerant and exclusive as those religions I criticized. In fact, I was much more intolerant than I am now as an evangelical Christian. If you've only ever known one world view, mine being secular, you find it difficult to see the prejudices and biases of your own way of thinking. Now, I don't think a pluralist is any less narrow or dogmatic than someone who practices one religion; these days they are often more so.

Some Christian books sparked a real interest in me. Most were by liberal writers, who have very different ideas about faith than I have now. However, they were enough to spark an interest in Jesus, and because they shared some of my secular views about the world, they spoke to me. In particular, a book by Brian McLaren called *The Secret Message of Jesus* really inspired me. It provided a vision of God changing the world through our actions, which appealed to the left-wing politics that I held. I started to become more interested in Jesus and I started to attend church.

INVESTIGATING CHRISTIANITY

At first I went to a local United Reformed Church, which was very liberal. It was a large family church, with a very pleasant and kind vicar. He gave a sermon on divorce, explaining that the reason Jesus didn't like it, or would prohibit it, is that it involves a lot of pain for the human beings involved.

This was a new concept to me. The idea that these religious morals or laws that I perceived as judgmental could actually be about our well-being had never occurred to me before. I had just perceived people who held them as arrogant and hypocritical. But I started to look on them in a new light; as protective boundaries that were there because God loved us. That really was a revelation. But now I look on all the supposedly 'outdated' or judgmental teachings of the church as protective. Adultery, promiscuity, greed and selfishness are rampant, and they cause a great deal of pain and sadness. I believe that is why God would not want people to take part – because they hurt people.

Then I started attending an ultra-liberal Anglican church, where many people who went were also Buddhists, or gay, or they had been hurt by churches they had attended in the past. It was a peculiar church, looking back, but God was definitely at work in it, and people developed and found faith. I felt a loving presence which I would now identify as the Holy Spirit – the living presence of God among us.

And so, gradually, I started to open up to Christianity as a way of love, a way that answered some of the questions and desires that I had had all my life. I loved Jesus' words in the Gospels – they resonated with my sense of right and wrong, justice and fairness. I made a decision to follow Christ.

I then started – very hesitantly – to attend some evangelical churches in the area. I have to say I wasn't impressed with some, which seemed to be very dogmatic and not very concerned about the world around them. There was more style than substance in a lot of them, I thought. But in others, there was a lot that interested me. I found a large evangelical Anglican church, which was quite conservative, but I thought it must be OK, because it has a large homelessness project.

I loved the worship music, which lifted my spirit and filled me with love as I praised the God that I was coming to know. And the teaching intrigued me. In particular, I remember a sermon that was about how God could clean out the anger, the sin and the pain within a person, through His Holy Spirit. Again, this was a new concept for me, but it was one that resonated deeply. I had thought the answer to the world's problems was psychological therapy, but here was someone telling me that it didn't require a psychology degree, or anything else fancy, to find healing. It just required faith and trust in God.

And (more to the point) it could deal with the bad stuff inside of me. I think as I was encountering the goodness of God, I started to be more aware of the negativity within me, the anger, the fear and the pain. Generally, this stuff gets covered up and repressed, and people try to ignore the demons within. The revelation wasn't negative, though, because I was being offered hope – the news that God loved me and could deal with this stuff. So I was getting a sense of the sin within, but not in a condemning or judgmental sense – it was in the context of being healed, of Jesus as the healer. I was starting to feel God's love.

Slowly, slowly, I opened up to God and to His Son, Jesus. I read the Bible regularly, and different kinds of Christian books. I still struggled with doubt. The concept of a supernatural, all-powerful God was difficult to accept, so steeped was I in the materialism of our culture. Where was God? Why couldn't we see God, why wasn't He physical?

One day I started reading the story of an atheist arts professor called Howard Storm, who had a near-death experience and went through some kind of a hellish existence. He called out to God and Jesus came to him. His was the most dramatic kind of conversion experience; he is now a pastor and his life is totally transformed.

What interested me was the way in which he described Jesus, and what Jesus had told him. It was all about love. Some of it seemed a little bit unorthodox for Christian teaching, though I've since talked to him, and he's got a pretty straightforward faith. I was totally fascinated. When I read the book now, I see how much of what was said was in the Bible. It opened my mind to the reality of a spiritual realm and the realization that nothing I knew actually contradicted that reality.

CAPTIVATED BY LOVE

Shortly after that, I was reading the Bible on my bed one day, and I had the most incredible experience of God's love. It was indescribable, incomparable to what I had known before in my life. And there was a strange sensation as I was feeling this love. I felt that the love was so strong that if a man was standing in front of me with a knife, about to kill me, that the love would be there regardless of that hate, regardless of the loss of my life. I knew this was God's love for all people.

Even though we hate God and do wrong and even hang Him on a cross, He loves us anyway. From that point on, there has not been a time when I have doubted the reality of God's existence.

I did struggle with the concept of the cross. Why couldn't God just forgive us anyway? How could all the sins of all the world be atoned for at one point in space and time? I prayed about it a lot, because all these Christians I was meeting up with seemed to see it as so important. I decided to choose to accept it, but it took some more steps in my journey before I really felt in my heart the absolute importance of the cross to a human being. Although I was aware that I did sin, and I asked for forgiveness for these sins, there was a further step I needed to take – one which I don't think is always taught in the Christian walk. That was surrendering to God's will.

The most obvious area in my life where this was not the case was relationships. I had a very secular, liberal approach to sex and love. I thought that anything goes as long as you're not hurting someone, which is the prevailing wisdom in my generation. What I wasn't fully aware of at the time is how much sex outside of committed relationships does hurt people, nor how most of what passes for 'love' in the world is nothing of the sort. Instead it is pure selfishness – the gratification of desires, whether romantic or sexual.

Ultimately, my life had been about searching for love, though I was not always conscious of that. Although there were many things that I would use to attempt to fill that gap – from the thrill of journalism to the stupor of the pint to the frisson from getting attention or admiration – they were not getting to the root of the matter. I wanted to be loved. And, in truth, I had rarely received that in my life before God came in.

But I had the idea in my mind that one has to be in a romantic relationship to be fully loved. Sadly, this is a very prevalent attitude in our culture and even in the church. There is so little community that the only point of intimacy and fellowship is in the biological nuclear family, the foundation of which is seen to be a romantic relationship.

But also my personal experience is that it is only a truly intimate relationship with Christ that really satisfies our desires. And without that relationship with the ultimate source of love, intimacy with others can be difficult and warped. Much of it is needy and selfish, particularly related to sexual desire.

Now I observe the objectification and idolization of people for their body shape or physical attributes with horror, though our culture is absolutely steeped in it. I think now that this is the very opposite of love and actually stifles the ability to love. Even in relationships, I see that people (including myself) are more concerned about their own needs than the other person – more concerned about receiving than giving and giving only to receive. It's so ingrained in our culture that it takes quite a long time to be aware of it, and it's still an ongoing and difficult process to remove it and to love instead.

So I wrestled between a biblical understanding of relationships and what I wanted, which was a partner. I got into some pretty ungodly relationships in the early days of being a Christian. But the issue really came to a head when I got involved with a guy who was not a Christian and who was struggling, and not in the best place after separating from his wife when she left him for someone else. But I was more concerned about my own emotional needs than his. When the relationship ended, I was really angry with God. For some reason, it was as if all the pain of my life that had been bottled up came out with a rush. I raged at God; why does He allow us to experience hurt? Why is this world so full of suffering and selfishness? Why, why, why?

SURRENDER

I had a choice at this point that I felt clearly within my soul – to choose Christ or to rebel.

I chose Christ and I surrendered my life, choosing to trust Him in everything. And this brought healing.

From this point came significant spiritual growth; I started to really know God. It was not easy and I didn't find that all of the people in church have really trodden this path. Allowing God to really reveal the truth within, to express deeply held emotions and share them with others, I was able to open up and allow the Holy Spirit to minister to me. By giving up my life to God and resolving to do His will only, I was being given freedom and a much more fulfilling life in return.

Because I was feeling the love and grace of God, I became more able to acknowledge my part in my own problems. I was able to fully acknowledge the sin in my heart and to truly ask forgiveness and repent. I became able to really trust God, that whatever happens, He is good, even if I don't have full understanding of why. I became more humble and aware that I was not as clever as I thought I was. The crucible of emotional pain can lead to really great riches in Christ, as anyone who has found them will testify.

So instead of questioning God's ways, I asked God to show me which way He wanted me to go. And the cross became ever more real to me, as my only hope of knowing goodness and righteousness. My ways were generally selfish and mean, but God's ways are wonderful. But it's only through the righteousness of Christ that we can follow them, through His taking our sin and pain upon Himself.

As my heart has felt more of God's love, and as my eyes have been opened to the deep problems of the world, I have been given more compassion for people. Whereas before I would get angry about the poverty and injustice, and criticize those whom I judged to be the cause of the problems, now God has inspired me to act on these issues. And I do less blaming of certain people, because I see the problem within all human hearts – hate, lust and greed – all are opposing God's will. It is through love that the world can be changed, and love ultimately comes from God through Christ. That is what I have experienced for myself.

These days, I'm an evangelical who is fairly conservative, although I'm open-minded on some points, and also strongly influenced by the charismatics' desire for a passionate intimacy with Christ, and I respect the concern for the suffering of the more liberal wing of the church. I have to thank liberal Christians for being my gateway to Jesus, but I have found that the only way to really receive the riches of the Bible is to accept it as God's Word and ask Jesus to teach me through it. It has become the living Word of God to me; I can't count the number of times I have felt God speaking to me through it.

A RATIONAL FAITH

I love using my brain and my love of investigating for truth in the field of apologetics – exploring the rational arguments for the Christian faith. Although my walk towards Christ was mainly an emotional one, my naturally questioning mind meant I had many doubts, and thinking through them was an important part of my walk. I've also found that you can be fully intellectually satisfied as a Christian.

In fact, there has been a revolution in Christian philosophy and biblical scholarship that means that evangelical belief has a rational basis, and the work of people like Alister McGrath, John Lennox and William Lane Craig has really enriched my faith.

I also talk a lot to atheists. Of course, some are atheists because of rational reasons, though often I find that they have heard only one half of the story. But some of them are so angry. Frequently they talk about God as though He is real, but it's just that they don't like Him. That makes me sad, because the God I know is full of love.

I also find it sad that the Bible gets such a bad press. Through the pages of the Bible, I have found the most wonderful insights into life – human nature, my problems and opportunities, my soul and well-being. I have found God's deep concern and compassion for those who are suffering in our world. Frequently when something is on my mind and I have a problem or I pray specifically about something, I open the Bible and the answer is staring me in the face.

The Bible is often criticized for the slaughter passages or laws that seem out of date to people today. When I approached the Bible with the intention of casting judgment on it I didn't get much out of it. If I came to it with the question, 'What is God wanting to teach me?', then I would get a much greater understanding. I have found that it has helped mould me to be a better person, a more loving person, and to be much closer to God.

As I look through the history of the human race, I see that it has done the same for many people over the years, particularly through the Victorian social reformers who did so much to improve our society. I look at the stories and see and relate to how God has driven them to care for the world through the Scriptures.

I love the story of William Wilberforce, although biographies do not always quite seem to capture how much of his work to abolish the slave trade was inspired by his passionate Christian faith.

I read about Victorian campaigner Josephine Butler, who hated sexual sin but who went into the workhouses to try to rescue prostitutes from their terrible lives, even inviting them into her own home. She also campaigned against draconian laws that oppressed these women.

When I read the writing and work of Martin Luther King and his peaceful and brave opposition to racism, I see his knowledge of the Bible all over it. God's Word can achieve great things when human beings seek to obey it and seek to follow God's will through it.

I've also found it important to seek the presence of God in my prayer – to be truthful and honest before Him, recognizing the faults and barriers to love that are in me, and asking for forgiveness. Although I'm generally a kinder and more patient person than I was before, I am very far from perfect and I mess up regularly. Selfishness and pride are probably the two main barriers to God in my own life; still He offers grace and redemption each time I ask for it, and slowly I'm learning a better way.

I'm also (very) slowly learning how to accept and love other people with all their faults. Although this is where I fail most regularly, it's also probably the most important lesson: to show the grace and forgiveness that I have received myself. Sometimes I feel God's love and it brings joy to my life. There has been so much healing too – some of it I never even knew that I needed. But now as I go around I see so much anger and pain in people's hearts and I wish for them that they could know the healing power of Jesus. It's available to everyone and His love is for all.

So for anyone reading this who does not know how much they are loved, I really recommend that you start asking, questioning, and opening your mind. Our culture teaches us a lot of lies about God, about love, and about what is good. But truth is out there and it's more amazing than you could possibly imagine.

I have been on a fantastic journey, and it has been worth every minute. I just thank Jesus for His love for me and I hope you will make the same discovery: that you are truly, deeply and passionately loved.

11

AN EVANGELIST
explains why he is not an Atheist[1]

Ravi Zacharias

Arriving home, a university student tells his parents that, after reading a popular atheist's book, he has renounced his family's faith. His mother is devastated by the news. The father struggles to engage his son in discussion, but to no avail. Soon this family that was once close and peaceable is now broken and hostile. Mother and son exchange abusive words with increasing intensity, and the siblings blame their brother's new strident atheism for their family's rift. After a night of arguing and pleading unsuccessfully with her son to reconsider his position, the mother takes an overdose of prescription medication and ends her life, unable to accept what she interprets to be the destruction of her family.

Although this particular scenario is imaginary, I suspect that in some measure similar scenes have played out more than a few times since the publication of Sam Harris's *Letter to a Christian Nation* and others by the so-called New Atheists. With Richard Dawkins and the late Christopher Hitchens, he calls for the banishment of all religious belief. 'Away with this nonsense!' is their battle cry. In

---

1   This chapter was excerpted and adapted from *The End of Reason* by Ravi Zacharias (Zondervan, 2008).

return, they promise a world of new hope and unlimited horizons – once we have shed this delusion of God.

I have news for them – news to the contrary. The reality is that the emptiness that results from the loss of the transcendent is stark and devastating, both philosophically and existentially. On the first day of a lectureship I held at Oxford University, the Oxford newspaper carried the story of the suicide of the student body president of an area college. After my lecture at the town hall that morning, I cannot begin to tell you the number of students who came to me to say that suicide is something they have considered.

In my travels across the globe, I have found this scenario to be conspicuous among our youth in universities everywhere as these institutions deliver meaninglessness in large doses. On campus after campus, in culture after culture, I have listened for hours to intellectuals, young and old, who testify to a deep-seated emptiness. Young, honest minds seek answers and meaning. No amount of philosophizing about a world without God brings hope. After four decades of covering every continent and delivering scores of university lectures, I have seen that this sense of alienation and meaninglessness is the principal malady of young minds. Academic degrees have not removed the haunting specter of the pointlessness of existence in a random universe. This deep malady of the soul will not be cured by the writings of the New Atheists. The momentary euphoria that may initially accompany a proclamation of liberation soon fades, and one finds oneself in the vice-like grip of despair in a life without ultimate purpose.

I was born to Indian parents and raised in India. My ancestors were priests from the highest caste of Hinduism in India's deep south. Religion is embedded in that culture and India has probably spawned more religions than any other nation on earth. Hinduism alone boasts 330 million gods in its pantheon. Consequently, a lifetime of watching ceremony, ritual, superstition and all that goes along with that world view made me totally reject all belief in the supernatural. Many times I wondered how people could actually believe what they said they did, and I marveled at the masses' apparent commitment to gullibility. On this I agree with the New Atheists.

People often say that India is the most religious country in the world. It may be true, yet many in India live as practical atheists. I was one of them. I found religion to be an utter bore. Listening to priests – whether Hindu, Buddhist, Christian, or other – chanting what seemed to me to be inanities made me long to escape their so-called hallowed buildings. I saw their beliefs as superstition and fear-mongering, a means of boosting the egos of the perpetrators and controlling their followers, for a mantra repeated often enough eventually becomes indispensable to existence. Modern-day 'guruism', especially of what I call the export variety, thrives in India today because the secularism exemplified in Europe and exported to the world leaves the inner person bankrupt and vulnerable to all kinds of beliefs. In Nietzschean terms, to me God was a manufactured entity. That was it, plain and simple.

Albert Camus begins his essay, *The Myth of Sisyphus*, with these words: 'There is only one really serious philosophical question, and that is suicide. Judging whether life is or is not worth living amounts to answering the fundamental question of philosophy.'[2] It is a haunting question; in fact, as I followed atheism to its logical conclusion in my own life, it became my question. Tragically, two of my close friends at college had already succeeded in their suicide attempts – one the heir to a highly successful business, the other a person who acted out of sheer aimlessness. Then it was my turn – a botched attempt in which I ended up in a hospital room in New Delhi, with doctors battling to keep me alive. It was in that lowly condition that I was handed a Bible, and the story of the gospel was read to me. All I can say now is how grateful I am that Richard Dawkins was not my mentor, for my life would have ended there and then. Instead, I trusted the Christ of the Scriptures, and today, having traveled this globe dozens of times, I find Jesus to be more beautiful and attractive than ever before.

---

2   Albert Camus, *The Myth of Sisyphus and Other Essays* (New York: Vintage, 1991), p. 3.

This means absolutely nothing to the New Atheists. But to me, to my family, and, I dare say, to tens of thousands of others in whose lives God has given me a small share, it has spelled the difference between despair and hope. This Jesus, whom I encountered in a moment of experience, I have tested through years of study and of seeking understanding. His description of the nature of reality and of everything within my own heart conforms to every test for truth to which I have submitted the teaching. I am as sure of my experience with Him as I am of my own existence. It is little wonder that the common people of Jesus' day heard Him gladly, and that when those marginalized by society were brought to Him for judgment, He spoke words of comfort and indicted their accusers.

For many years I have studied, researched, and written about the world's religions. But just to be fair to atheism, I walked the extra mile. As a visiting scholar at Cambridge University, I studied under a minister-turned-atheist, Don Cupitt, who was then dean of one of the colleges. Ironically, as an ordained Anglican priest, he was better known for his denial of God than for his service to God. I chose to study under him because I wanted to understand the case for atheism from a valid source. I wanted to hear and understand the full share of the argument for atheism once more, in case I had missed anything when I was younger. I have since read the writings of the New Atheists and their perspective of a world without God.

WE ALL START WITH QUESTIONS

Where do I begin to unpack the systemic contradictions of the atheistic world view? Perhaps the best starting point would be to tell you why I am not an atheist. To begin, everyone has a world view. A world view basically offers answers to four necessary questions – questions that relate to *origin, meaning, morality, and hope that assures a destiny*. These answers must be correspondingly true and, as a whole, coherent.

Origin

How did life come to be?

Big Bang cosmology, along with Einstein's theory of general relativity, implies that there is indeed an 'in the beginning'.[3] All the data indicate a universe that is exploding outward from a point of infinite density. We know quite well that this singularity is not really a point; it is the whole of three-dimensional space compressed to zero size. This, in fact, actually represents a boundary at which space ceases to exist. Even the terms plead for explanation. The point I wish to make here (if you'll pardon the pun) is that at the point of the universe's origin, there is *something* rather than *nothing* – a mystery that leaves science totally silent.

Not only is there something; the laws of science actually break down right at the beginning. The very starting point for an atheistic universe is based on something that cannot explain its own existence. The scientific laws by which atheists want all certainty established do not even exist as a category at the beginning of the universe because, according to those laws of science by which atheists want to measure all things, matter cannot simply 'pop into existence' on its own.

The silence from atheistic science on why there is something rather than nothing is deafening. Atheistic philosopher Bertrand Russell said that the universe is 'just there'.[4] But that clearly is not

---

3   Unless, of course, Harris wants to philosophize, as theoretical physicist Stephen Hawking does, about a universe without boundary or edge and go the route of a 'world ensemble cosmology' and imaginary time. John Polkinghorne who was Professor of Mathematical Physics at Queens' College, Cambridge, a colleague of Hawking, had just one response to that proposition for those of us studying under him: 'Let's recognize imagination for what it is.' (The quote is from my class notes, but I found a similar statement in his book *One World: The Interaction of Science and Theology* [London: SPCK, 1986], p. 80: 'Let us recognize these speculations for what they are. They are not physics but, in the strictest sense, metaphysics.') Hawking does grant a 'beginning'. He just lacks a beginning point. In his extensions, Hawking is simply engaging in bad metaphysics.

4   A transcript of the 1948 debate between Bertrand Russell and Father Frederick C. Copleston is available online; see http://www.philvaz.com/apologetics/p20.htm (accessed 25 February 2013). This conversation appears under the heading, 'The Argument from Contingency'.

a scientific explanation. According to science, nothing that exists (or that is) can explain its own existence. Yet, according to their cosmology, we just happen to be. This means that any *purpose* for our being is as random as any *cause* for our being.

The vacuousness of the atheistic approach to the universe's origin is illustrated by Nobel laureate and atheist Francis Crick's answer to the question of how life around us began: 'Probably because a spaceship from another planet brought spores to seed the earth.'[5] Carl Sagan went to his grave 'viewing the whole universe as nothing more than molecules in motion.'[6] He believed that some extraterrestrial entity would be able to explain us to ourselves and thereby justified the billions of dollars spent on listening in on outer space, watching and waiting for some contact.[7]

However, Donald Page of Princeton's Institute for Advanced Science has calculated the odds against our universe randomly taking a form suitable for life as one out of $10,000,000,000^{124}$ – a number that exceeds all imagination.[8] Astronomers Fred Hoyle and N. C. Wickramasinghe found that the odds of the random formation of a single enzyme from amino acids anywhere on our planet's surface are one in 10^{20}. Furthermore, they observe: 'The trouble is that there are about two thousand enzymes and the chance of obtaining them all in a random trial is only one part in $(10^{20})20,000 = 10^{40,000}$, ... an outrageously small probability that could not be faced even if the whole universe consisted of organic soup.'[9] And this is just one step in the formation of life. Nothing has yet been said about DNA and where it came from, or of the

---

5   Quoted in Michael J. Behe, *Darwin's Black Box: The Biochemical Challenge to Evolution*, 10th anniversary ed. (New York: Free Press, 2006), p. 248. Francis Crick is the co-discoverer of the structure of the DNA molecule.

6   Quoted in Philip Graham Ryken, *Jeremiah and Lamentations: From Sorrow to Hope* (Wheaton, Ill.: Crossway, 2001), p. 100.

7   See Carl Sagan, 'The Quest for Extraterrestrial Intelligence', *Cosmic Search* 1 (1978), http://www.bigear.org/vol1no2/sagan.htm.

8   Cited in William Lane Craig, 'In Defence of Rational Theism', in *Does God Exist? The Great Debate*, ed. J. P. Moreland and Kai Nielsen (Nashville: Nelson, 1990), p. 143.

9   ibid.

transcription of DNA to RNA, which scientists admit cannot even be numerically computed. Nor has anything been said of mitosis or meiosis. One would have to conclude that the chance of the random ordering of organic molecules is not essentially different from a big fat zero. Perhaps that's why they call it a singularity, because it is without definition or empirical explanation.

That's the zero to which the New Atheists give credit for everything. And if one accepts this explanation, the resulting pointlessness of existence is devastating to our hunger for significance. When it suits the atheist, only intelligence can explain intelligibility, but when it is discomforting, primordial self-existent soup will do. They cannot hide their prejudices.

I want to add that our arguments for the existence of God do not hinge on debunking evolution. Evolution is a straw man that has been thrown up, as if all that needs to be done to achieve the crashing down of belief in God is to posit evolution. Serious intellectuals ought to know that no world view is established on one knockout argument. In *Miracles*, C. S. Lewis takes this kind of thinking to task: 'Reason might conceivably be found to depend on [another reason] and so on; it would not matter how far this process was carried provided you found Reason coming from Reason at each stage. It is only when you are asked to believe in Reason coming from non-reason that you must cry Halt.'[10]

Meaning

If life is random, then the inescapable consequence, first and foremost, is that there can be no ultimate meaning and purpose to existence. This consequence is the existential Achilles heel of atheistic belief. As individuals and collectively as cultures, we humans long for meaning. But if life is random, we have climbed the evolutionary ladder only to find nothing at the top.

Author and satirist G. K. Chesterton remarked that meaninglessness does not come from being weary of pain but from being weary of pleasure. *Pleasure*, not pain, is the death knell of meaning.

---

10   C. S. Lewis, *Miracles* (New York: Macmillan, 1978), pp. 27-8.

Our problem is not that pain has produced emptiness in our lives; the real problem is that even pleasure ultimately leaves us empty and unfulfilled. When the pleasure button is pressed incessantly, we are left feeling bewilderingly empty and betrayed.

The greatest disappointment (and resulting pain) you can feel is when you have just experienced that which you thought would bring you the ultimate in pleasure – and it has let you down. Pleasure without boundaries produces a life without purpose. That is real pain. No death, no tragedy, no atrocity – *nothing* really matters. Life is sheer hollowness, with no purpose. As a suicide note left by a man in Las Vegas, the city of glitz and gambling, stated, 'Here there are no answers.'[11]

Contrary to the New Atheists, at least writers such as Voltaire, Sartre and Nietzsche were honest and consistent in their views. They admitted the ridiculousness of life, the pointlessness of everything in an atheistic world. Contemporary atheists, however, are so blind to the conceit of their own minds that they try to present this view of life as some sort of triumphal liberation. Sartre, as atheistic intellectual elites know but are embarrassed to acknowledge, denounced atheism on his deathbed as philosophically unlivable.[12]

Some years ago, in a debate between atheism and Christianity, Antony Flew described a Christian philosopher's experience of knowing Christ as 'grotesque'.[13] But Flew vacated the atheistic

---

11   Adam Goldman, 'The Suicide Capital of America', AP News, 9 February 2004, http://www.cbsnews.com/stories/2004/02/09/health/main599070.shtml   (accessed 17 September 2007)

12   See Thomas Molnar, 'Jean-Paul Sartre, RIP: A Late Return', *National Review* 34 (11 June 1982): 677: 'It is sufficient to quote a single sentence from what Sartre said then to measure the degree of his acceptance of the grace of God and the creatureliness of man: "I do not feel that I am the product of chance, a speck of dust in the universe, but someone who was expected, prepared, prefigured. In short, a being whom only a Creator could put here; and this idea of a creating hand refers to God."' Quoted in Josh McDowell and Don Stewart, *Existentialism*, http://www.greatcom.org/resources/secular_religions/ch04/default.htm (accessed 1 October 2007)

13   Antony Flew, 'The Case for God Challenged', in *Does God Exist?*, p. 167. Flew writes: '[J. P.] Moreland's appeal to his 'personal experiences' strikes me as absolutely grotesque.'

camp, no longer able to honestly justify its metaphysical moorings. Before he died, he declared his belief in God, albeit as a distant god who takes no active part in the lives of men and women.

Morality

Not only does atheism's world view lead to the death of meaning; it also leads to the death of moral reasoning.

Sam Harris argues in *Letter to a Christian Nation* that examples of God's failure to protect humanity are to be seen everywhere, such as the massive destruction in the city of New Orleans brought about by a hurricane in 2005. What was God doing while Katrina laid waste to New Orleans, he asks? Didn't he hear the prayers of those who 'fled the rising waters for the safety of their attics, only to be slowly drowned there'? These people, Harris insists, 'died talking to an imaginary friend.'[14]

But when Harris accuses God of such destruction or asks why God does not prevent the rape, torture, and murder of children[15], what is he *really* saying? Is he saying that such things are evil, ought to be evil, or ought not to be allowed by a loving God? In any of the three assertions he is at best saying, 'I do not see a moral order at work here.' But if there is no God, who has the authority to say whether there is a moral order in operation? Sam Harris? Adolf Hitler? *Who*?

In addition to hitting God for hurricanes, rape, torture, and murder, Harris lays the Holocaust at the door of medieval Christianity. Harris's view is basically that the anti-Semitism spawned by Christians during medieval times led to the Holocaust at the hands of the Nazis.[16] But has he read about Hitler's own spiritual journey? Has he read anything about Hitler's dabbling in the occult? Is he aware that Hitler personally presented the writings of Nietzsche to Stalin and Mussolini? Is he ignoring the fact that others who were not Jewish were also slaughtered by Hitler? Did

---

14   Sam Harris, *Letter to a Christian Nation* (New York: Knopf, 2006), p. 52.

15   ibid., p. 51.

16   ibid., pp. 41-42.

he read Nazi mastermind Adolf Eichmann's last words that refused repentance and denied belief in God? Does he know how many Russians were killed by the Nazi machine? Does he know that Hitler's point was that the destruction of the weak is a good thing for the survival of the strong and that 'nature intended it that way,' as is taught by atheistic evolution's tenet of natural selection – 'the survival of the fittest'? None of these signs of the Holocaust point back to Christianity.

For Harris to convince us that Hitler was wrong to do what he did, he has to borrow from an objective moral framework to support his point. Let me put it another way. If Harris's assertion that no moral order is visible in the world is true, we may well ask why Hitler couldn't introduce his own order. What was wrong with what he did? What is the basis on which Harris is calling Hitler immoral? Or is he calling him immoral?

How conveniently the atheist plays word games! When it is Stalin or Pol Pot who does the slaughtering, it is because they are deranged or irrational ideologues; their atheism has nothing to do with their actions. But when a Holocaust is engendered by an ideologue, it is the culmination of 400 years of Christian intolerance for the Jew. Atheists can't have it both ways. If the murder of innocents is wrong, it is wrong not because science tells us it is wrong but because every life has intrinsic worth – a postulate that atheism simply cannot deduce. There is no way for Harris as an atheist to argue for moral preferences except by his own subjective means, that is, his personal preference or environment. One cannot make absolute statements based on one's personal feelings on a matter. That fact provides the very reason his own genre of writers within naturalism's frame of reference[17] admit that moral reasoning is not rational apart from God. Their philosophical word games are nothing more than an attempt to escape the stifling unreason to which they are driven.

What is the objective moral framework Harris adopts on which he has built his entire critique of God? His emotion-laden critique

---

17   Naturalism's assumption is that nature is all we have.

hangs on an argument that says: 'I can see no moral framework operating in the world, but what I do see is morally condemnable.' In philosophical terms, this is called a mutually exclusive assumption. Therefore, the moral framework he is forced to adopt is, in reality, one he built himself.

Given this, it is little wonder that Bertrand Russell admitted he couldn't live as though ethical values were simply a matter of personal taste and that he therefore found his own views 'incredible'. 'I do not know the solution', he said.[18] In an earlier debate with Jesuit priest Frederick Copleston, Russell had tried another route to get around objective morality and ended up looking bad. When Copleston asked him how he differentiated between good and bad, Russell answered: 'I don't have any justification any more than I have when I distinguish between blue and yellow ... I can see they are different.'

'Well, that is an excellent justification, I agree,' said Copleston. 'You distinguish blue and yellow by seeing them, so you distinguish good and bad by what faculty?'

'By my feelings', was Russell's reply.[19]

Father Copleston was kind. The next question was staring Russell in the face but wasn't asked because he already looked so weak in that part of the discussion. The question that should have been asked was, 'Mr Russell, in some cultures they love their neighbours; in other cultures they eat them. Do you have a personal preference, and if so, what is it?'

Russell's agnosticism and ambiguity about his own views on ethical values were at least more honest than Harris's morality concocted in his own mind – as if morality should be self-evident to everybody, regardless of whether God exists or not. Harris's antagonism toward God ends up proving that he intuitively finds some things reprehensible. But he cannot explain his innate sense of right and wrong – the reality of God's law written on his heart

---

18   Bertrand Russell, letter to the editor, *The Observer* (London), 6 October 1957.

19   For this exchange between Copleston and Russell, see Al Seckel, ed., *Bertrand Russell on God and Religion*, pp. 138-9. For a transcript of this debate, see footnote 4 of this chapter.

– because there is no logical explanation for how that intuition toward morality could develop from sheer matter and chemistry.

Popularly stated, I would put it in this way:

- when you assert that there is such a thing as evil, you must assume there is such a thing as good;

- when you say there is such a thing as good, you must assume there is a moral law by which to distinguish between good and evil. There must be some standard by which to determine what is good and what is evil;

- when you assume a moral law, you must posit a moral lawgiver – the source of the moral law;

- But this moral lawgiver is precisely whom atheists are trying to disprove.

Now Harris and other atheists may protest, 'Why is a moral lawgiver necessary in order to recognize good and evil?' For the simple reason that a moral affirmation cannot remain an abstraction. The person who moralizes assumes intrinsic worth in himself or herself and transfers intrinsic worth to the life of another, and thus he or she considers that life worthy of protection (as in the illustrations Harris gives, namely, rape, torture, murder, and natural catastrophes). Transcending value must come from a person of transcending worth. But in a world in which matter alone exists there can be no intrinsic worth. Let me put it in philosophical terms:

- objective moral values exist only if God exists;

- objective moral values do exist (a point Harris concedes in his letter);

- therefore God exists.

An examination of these premises and their validity presents a very strong argument for the existence of God. In fact, J. L. Mackie, a vociferous atheist who challenged the existence of God on the basis of the reality of evil, granted at least this logical connection when he said: 'We might well argue ... that objective, intrinsically prescriptive features, supervenient upon natural ones, constitute so odd a cluster of qualities and relations that they are most unlikely to have arisen in the ordinary course of events, without an all-powerful God to create them.'[20]

Therefore, we must agree with the conclusion that *nothing can be intrinsically prescriptively good unless there also exists a God who has fashioned the universe thus.* But this is the very Being atheists deny exists because of the existence of evil.

Indeed, Harris clearly assumes that God kills innocent people, and thus He is violating His own laws. Let's grant this for a moment. Why is killing innocents wrong? Is it wrong because God says so? Is it wrong because Harris believes that an innocent ought not to be killed? If we assume the first, namely, it is wrong because God says it is wrong, then God contradicts Himself through his actions – saying it is wrong but killing innocents anyway. Harris, however, is not relieved of the responsibility of proving his argument that innocents ought not to be killed. To genuinely believe this he must assume a moral framework that supports the intrinsic value of innocent life. But based on his atheistic starting point, he has no grounds for such a moral framework.

This leaves us with a third option – one that Harris has completely ignored or refused to consider: he is selectively borrowing from the biblical revelation of justice and retribution while ignoring the big story into which it fits and by which it gains its purpose. His moral argument distorts the Bible's finer points while denying its big picture.

Christianity teaches that every single life has ultimate value. In secularism, while there is no ultimate value to a life, the atheist subjectively selects particular values to applaud. This game is played every day by the relativist camp, while it refuses to allow the other side the benefit of playing by the same rules.

Hope
What else dies in atheism? Hope.

If there's one recurring theme I have heard in my three decades of travelling the world, it is the longing of the human heart for hope.

---

20   Quoted in J. P. Moreland, 'Reflections on Meaning in Life without God', *Trinity Journal* NS9 (1988), p. 14.

Devoid of reasons for hope, people will create substitutes and follow cultic rituals they have devised in anticipation of realizing hope.

What is the atheist's answer for hope in the ultimate stage of hopelessness, which is the way death is often seen? Nothing. Silence. The atheists' treatment of the subject of death is usually replete with debunkings of descriptions of 'near-death experiences', intended to dismiss any reality offered by the dying to those they are leaving behind. But how do they know these descriptions aren't true? One cannot, of course, just take utterances at face value, and so their scepticism is justified. But does it follow that oblivion or agnosticism is the only option?

This same kind of scepticism resided in some of the disciples, who did not believe at first that Jesus had risen from the dead. They had heard this kind of story before. They, too, had no clear understanding of what follows death and thought that perhaps Jesus' resurrection was some fanciful story conjured up by hallucinating women. I wonder whether multiple evidences that Jesus had risen from the dead, given to modern-day atheists, would make any difference. The apostle Peter saw more and was close to more of the miracles than almost any other disciple, yet when it mattered most, his faith struggled to survive.

The problem with evidence is that it is very much limited to the moment and creates the demand for more evidence. I have seen this in my own life over and over. Today it may be a failing business that is in need of God's intervention. Tomorrow I may want to be healed from cancer. The day after that, I may even want a loved one to be brought back from the dead.

The world view of the Christian faith is simple enough. God has put enough into this world to make faith in Him a most reasonable thing. But He has left enough out to make it impossible to live by sheer reason alone.

If the atheist is wrong, there is no hope or second chance to get it right. Consider the point of Pascal's wager. The French philosopher Blaise Pascal didn't say he was wagering his belief. He was essentially saying that there are two tests for belief: the empirical test – that which is based on investigation – and the existential test – that which is based on personal experience. By denying the existence of God, atheists leave themselves just one option in the pursuit of happiness and purpose, namely, the existential test of self-fulfillment.

For the believer in God and the follower of Jesus, there is more than the existential test, which is subject to circumstance and condition. We also have the empirical test of the person, teaching, and work of Jesus Christ. Atheists may respond by saying there is an empirical test for the naturalist as well, one who believes in matter alone. But on issues of morality and meaning they have nothing to look to for a moral framework beyond themselves, and if their assumptions are true, the existential arena is the only legitimate route for the pursuit for meaning. Pascal was declaring that if the existential test for finding meaning in life was the only option left to him, the hungers of his heart had been met in following Jesus and thus he was fulfilled. In a worst-case scenario, where the atheist is right and death is oblivion, Pascal had still met the only test the atheist has for belief and had found his relationship with Jesus to be existentially fulfilling. As a Christian, he met both his own test for truth in the person of Jesus – the empirical test – *and* the existential test posed by the atheist. It was for that reason he could say he could not be a loser, and the gamble was not a gamble he could lose, no matter which test he used.

An Argument for God's Existence
Lastly, I want to briefly outline the case for the existence of God and the person of Jesus in particular. I borrow an argument – one of the least complicated from among the many – from a philosopher at the University of Southern California, Professor Dallas Willard. He takes a three-stage approach in his defence for the existence of God. (No, these are not proofs. Proof for metaphysical assertions is a misuse of the term.)

Routinely, three tests for truth are applied:

(1) logical consistency
(2) empirical adequacy
(3) experiential relevance.

When submitted to these tests, the Christian message meets the demand for truth. Willard's carefully constructed argument is posted on his website (www.dwillard.org), or you may read it in the book *Does God Exist?*[21] In the following sections, I will briefly paraphrase the argument.

In stage one, regardless of how physical, concrete reality is sectioned out, we end up with a state where the evidence of any physical entity explaining its own existence is zero. That said, we come to a real situation of determining how many series of causes it takes to explain all of existence. We cannot have an infinite series of causes in time, starting from the present of any completed state and moving backward in search of an ultimate cause, because if the sequence were infinite, we would never arrive at the present. And as already mentioned, nothing in this physical universe can explain its own existence, i.e., something does not come from nothing. Therefore, in order for there to be something (and there is), there must be at least one state that is self-existent and does not derive its existence from something else. And it must be something non-physical.

In this first stage of the argument, then, we have not posited a God; we have just posited a non-physical entity that explains its own existence and is uncaused.

In stage two of his argument, Willard posits the argument *to design*. The argument here is not of aesthetic design but of intelligent specificity. It is important to distinguish between the two. If you walked onto a distant planet and saw a million stones in a perfect triangle, you could, of course, argue that over millions of years this formation could have randomly happened in a pleasantly aesthetic way.

To even have the capacity to reason this far and to recognize the aesthetics of the arrangement of stones requires certain components

---

21   See Dallas Willard, 'Language, Being, God, and the Three Stages of Theistic Evidence', in *Does God Exist?* pp. 197-218.

or raw material – the 'alphabet' for life – that sets us apart from our environment. A can of alphabet soup dumped onto a table implies that somebody made that soup. You would absolutely deny that those shapes just happened to be in the soup. And if the letters fell out of the can in sequence every time, you would never even consider the possibility that it was accidental.

But suppose I took a trip to a distant planet and saw a crumpled piece of paper on which were written the words, 'Hello, Ravi, did you bring some curry and rice with you?' I would not in a million years conclude that this note was produced by the laws of physics. That note would have had to have been the result of intelligence, not chance. In the same way, the 'raw materials' that have resulted in this universe as we have it have been brought together simultaneously in the most amazing combinations – combinations too amazing to have just happened by accident. That is the argument *to design*.

Finally, stage three deals with the course of human events – historical, social, and individual. A look at human history – and specifically at the person and work of Jesus Christ – shows why He was who He claimed to be and why millions follow Him today. A comparison of Jesus, Muhammad, Krishna (if he ever actually lived), Buddha, and Mahavira quickly shows the profound differences in their claims and demonstrations. In fact, none I have mentioned here except Jesus even claimed to be divine. Krishna came the closest, but considering him in the context of the Vedas and the Gita, one cannot even be certain that he truly lived. It boils down to this: for the follower of Jesus Christ, the fact that the universe cannot explain itself, added to the obvious intelligence behind the universe, linked to the historical and experiential verification of what Jesus taught and did, make belief in Him a very rational and existentially fulfilling reality.

Contrary to the atheist's claim that followers of Jesus Christ live in a world of hocus-pocus, I think the reverse is true. It is naturalism – unreserved trust in scientific knowledge – that propagates a mystification of that world view in which only matter exists. C. S. Lewis observed:

There is something which unites magic and applied science while separating both from the 'wisdom' of earlier ages. For the wise men of old, the cardinal problem had been how to conform the soul to reality and the solution had been knowledge, self-discipline, and virtue. For magic and applied science alike the problem is how to subdue reality to the wishes of men: the solution is a technique.[22]

Origin, meaning, morality, and destiny – any world view must offer answers to these four necessary questions. These answers must be correspondingly true and, as a whole, coherent. The atheistic world view fails to offer coherent answers to these four questions. As such, atheists have left unaddressed how to persuade the human heart to do, and to *want* to do, that which is true, good, and beautiful. Yet the argument for the existence of God and the application of tests of truth to the message of the Christian gospel and its existential implications make for a reasonable and coherent world view.

---

22   C. S. Lewis, *The Abolition of Man* (New York: Macmillan, 1947), p. 48.

SOLAS
CENTRE FOR PUBLIC CHRISTIANITY

'Always be prepared to give an answer to everyone who asks you to give the reason for the hope that you have, but do this with gentleness and respect.' This admonition was given through Peter who, on a famous occasion (Mark 14:66-72), was rather unprepared to stand up for Jesus. But he was ransomed, healed, restored and forgiven, and he became a powerful witness and evangelist. Through his words, God calls His people to be prepared to share the good news that centres on the life, death and resurrection of Jesus Christ.

The ministry of **SOLAS – Centre for Public Christianity** is to give expression to the good news of that gospel in the public realm and to encourage and equip Christians to make open and public profession of their faith within the context of twenty-first-century European culture.

In response to those who seek to exclude Christianity from public life, SOLAS believes in the truth and contemporary relevance of the gospel. We believe that Europe was founded upon and largely owes its culture to Christianity, and that the current retreat from Christianity is leading to the breakdown of society and the collapse of family life. Secularism represents a backward step, and all the time Jesus offers fullness of life (John 10:10). We aim to enable people to reclaim this Christian heritage.

This involves vigorous public engagement on a number of fronts. SOLAS has been involved in public debates and conferences. We intend to provide good-quality training and resources, such as the recently published *Quest* (*Cafe Culture Evangelism*). We will encourage Christians and churches to use the arts, philosophy, music, history, society, media, medicine, science, theology and the community of the church to express and teach the Christian faith, as given to us in the Bible.

Our vision is for church-based persuasive evangelism, particularly focusing on sceptics, cultural influencers and critical thinkers. We want to engage in positive apologetics, addressing current issues and the intellectual struggles related to those concerns, as well as the humanitarian needs of those at risk within society.

Our goal is the spread of the gospel and the extension of Christ's kingdom.

Also available from Christian Focus ...

THE DAWKINS LETTERS
CHALLENGING ATHEIST MYTHS **DAVID ROBERTSON**

paperback ISBN 978-1-84550-597-4
epub ISBN 978-1-84550-652-0
Mobi ISBN 978-1-78191-027-6

The Dawkins Letters

David Robertson

When Richard Dawkins published *The God Delusion*, David Robertson wanted there to be an intelligent Christian response. After some ill-thought-through interventions in the media, it was obvious that no one was really going to answer the real issues, so David Robertson wrote an open letter to Richard Dawkins on his church website. This has found its way into Richard Dawkins' website, where it generated the largest response of any posting up to that time. Since then it has been the source of continued discussion – being a critical part of the largest discussion since that time as his book was officially reviewed on the website.

The ferocity of the responses and the shallowness of the thinking that it exhibited spurred David to write this book. Christians need to know where Dawkins is weak and we need to explain things better! It draws upon David's experience as a debater, letter writer, pastor and author.

This is a very honest book. It agrees with Dawkins where appropriate but also does not hesitate to point out where some of his thinking does not hold together – It is written in a gentle spirit of enquiry.

David Robertson is pastor of St Peter's Free Church of Scotland, Dundee.

The content is excellent. It's a fun, engaging read that seeks to be as charitable as possible (with an obviously virulent opponent) while not shrinking back from pointing out and exposing the fallacious, emotional and often childish arguments constantly employed by Dawkins.

Ligon Duncan, Chancellor and CEO, Reformed Theological Seminary

Comment about the initial 'Letter' that appeared on Richard Dawkins' website and which prompted the writing of the book: 'Wow, this is an intelligent and well-crafted view of RD's book.'

Response from an atheist on Richard Dawkins's Website

... probably the book's greatest triumph is that it doesn't come across as being a knee-jerk polemic right back at Dawkins, but rather a book that deals with bigger atheist arguments (myths) and as such has more value than just for the next few months.

Gary Aston, Youth Pastor, England

Christian Focus Publications

Our mission statement –

STAYING FAITHFUL

In dependence upon God we seek to impact the world through literature faithful to His infallible Word, the Bible. Our aim is to ensure that the Lord Jesus Christ is presented as the only hope to obtain forgiveness of sin, live a useful life and look forward to heaven with Him.

Our Books are published in four imprints:

CHRISTIAN FOCUS

popular works including biographies, commentaries, basic doctrine and Christian living.

CHRISTIAN HERITAGE

books representing some of the best material from the rich heritage of the church.

MENTOR

books written at a level suitable for Bible College and seminary students, pastors, and other serious readers. The imprint includes commentaries, doctrinal studies, examination of current issues and church history.

CF4•K

children's books for quality Bible teaching and for all age groups: Sunday school curriculum, puzzle and activity books; personal and family devotional titles, biographies and inspirational stories – Because you are never too young to know Jesus!

Christian Focus Publications Ltd,
Geanies House, Fearn, Ross-shire,
IV20 1TW, Scotland, United Kingdom.
www.christianfocus.com